Living in Harmony with Your Dog

text by Piero M. Bianchi
illustrations by Marisa Vestita

WHITE STAR PUBLISHERS

Contents

unwanted behavior is plain wrong, because your pet will take such a behavior as acceptable and therefore it can keep it for the future.

Most behavior pathologies tend to get considerably worse as time goes by and make living together with the pet more and more difficult, until leading little responsible people to euthanasia or abandonment.

According to recent research lead by an American team of veterinaries dog behaviorist, the most problematic issues for a dog owner are: aggressiveness (towards humans or other animals), acts of vandalism (destruction of objects or furniture), constant barking (especially at lonely times), inappropriate urination and defecation, phobias, excessive shyness, excessive sexual activity, and digging.

So, where to turn to heal a dog affected by behavioral disorders? The current qualified figure is the veterinary behaviorist: general practitioners aren't

1.
Choosing the Right Dog

Those who choose a dog as a friend and companion don't just share a house and a life, but they usually establish a long lasting partnership and research suggests that they benefit from the commitment on a psychical as well as on a physical level.

Starting from childhood, we must underline that, living with a dog, children establish an extremely important relationship, enriching themselves with several positive effects. Child psychologists highlight how dogs share with children their dependency from adults in order to survive. Growing up with a dog, the child will play different roles within the relationship, as being a parent, a peer and a son. Each step of the child development can be enriched by a dog, due to the endless shades of meaning that the pet can take on during his or her growing-up process. A dog, basically, acts as a security blanket: thanks to their emotional bond, the child perceives continuous assurance, reassurance which allow him or her to move forward both on a physical and psychical level, exorcising his or her fear of the unknown and strengthening his or her inner self with the otherness. Dogs are real life lessons: they allow children to become aware of their own existence as living being as well as of the duties and responsibilities of human beings. A dog, in fact, has to be fed, looked after, cleaned, and constantly monitored. The lessons, however, go even beyond that: in fact, animals come to life, grow up, get old, fall ill and die. In other words: they live.

Even in an adult context, living together with a dog can be an extremely enriching experience. An ethological Canadian research revealed that living with a dog represents an important prevention and therapy of all sorts of stressful circumstances as, for example, quarreling with neighbors, bad relationships with colleagues and superiors, health fears, conflicts with partners, traffic and so on. Carried out research points out that those who choose a dog as a friend differ from those who don't own any, in many crucial aspects: they consider their existence highly qualitative, don't experience continuous stress intensively, and face health as well as economic problems in a better way. They only occasionally suffer from psychosomatic

disorders (as, for example irritability, headache, heartburn, depression, circulatory disturbances, dermatological problems) and believe that life critical events (death, divorce, diseases) may be definitively lightened by living together with a pet. The elderly enjoy benefits as well: life quality enhancement and longer life have been acknowledged. More and more often, psychologists restate that taking care of a dog represents a panacea to reduce loneliness and prevents depression, increasing social skills. During this delicate stage of life, in fact, we experience a rarefaction of social relationships: that can lead the elderly to behavior disorders (mainly depression) and psychosomatic problems which mean their attempt to adapt to the situation. Well, it has been scientifically proved that a dog (and the need to take care of it) prevents such difficulties and removes them in case the disorders have already occurred. The elderly needs to love and the urgency to have someone to feel useful and responsible for can be fulfilled by a pet presence. Another very positive aspect is the physical stimulation coming from the relationship with a dog. Walking it several times a day commits oneself to move and fights sedentariness. It shouldn't surprise, therefore, that some American insurance companies have reduced health insurance premiums to elderly clients who live together with a four-footed friend. To confirm it, a group of researchers from Texas has proved how elderly people owning a dog seek their doctor's advice less frequently than their peer, used to live without pets.

Age

When we decide to buy a dog, one of the first question to be resolved is the pet age. Is it better to choose a young dog or an adult one? Managing a puppy involves a considerable practical and economic commitment: it has to be watched and taken care of, indeed. It has to be taught basic good manners rules, to learn sphincters control. It needs to play, to go out and walk often, to be fed several times a day. Without taking into account all medical procedures, such as veterinary examinations, vaccinations, deworming, and different kinds of checks. Breeding the pet, following its progress, teaching it the basics of behavior and human relationships, are fundamental steps to shape its character as well as a source of joy and satisfaction for the owner. A young dog or an adult one are definitively easier to manage (especially for time and attention to be devoted), but often give you less intense personal

satisfaction. Moreover, it must be taking into account that in most cases, adult dogs are less conditionable in terms of habits and behavior. Instead, if you have decided to get a puppy, the best age to include it in your family is between six and eight weeks, since – according to ethologists and dog psychologists – that is the age when puppies establish their first social relationships. A too early or a too late inclusion may cause problems and be the reason for behavior disorders in its adulthood. Scientific research within dog behavior during the last decades have clarified aspects in that regard. The puppies too much in contact with members of our species sometimes become hyper addicted to human beings, to the extent that when they become adults, they develop an antisocial behavior towards their counterparts (up to be sexually impotent).

On the contrary, the subjects that have never been in touch with human beings during their first three months of life, may become hardly socializable pets and, in some cases, it's almost impossible to make them domestic. Raising puppies with few human contacts during their socialization stage, may cause behavior disorders as for example, shyness or fear. Among the most common problems, it's worth referring to deprivation syndrome (a behavior disorder as a result of a prolonged absence of stimuli) arising from missing socialization after excess isolation: puppies turn out to be very scary in whatever circumstance, such as noises, other animal presence, contacts with strangers and so on.

Gender

Females are generally sweeter and more loving than males: therefore, those who choose to venture into living together with a dog and aim at structuring the relationship throughout tenderness and niceness, would rather opt for a female. Females, indeed, integrate themselves better into the household; they are patient, tolerant, caring and, though sterilized, they keep motherly instincts and can relate to children.

Male dogs, on their part, are more stubborn, determined and maybe more difficult to train. But they have a more solid character, predictable to some extent; that provides man dog relationships with features of steadiness and loyalty. A male can encounter problems in the hierarchical ladder of a family made of several elements, especially

if the family doesn't adopt uniform policies.

For the same reasons, single people or those who live on their own may prefer a male pet, especially if they want to make the connection exclusive. However, it must be taken into account that males may turn out to be more rebellious and aggressive with one another. That depends only partly on hormonal components. Therefore, surgical sterilization hardly ever mitigates the effect. Male physical presence may also make bigger subjects' restraint more problematic. Females, instead, are generally calmer, less troublemaker. They socialize more easily with other dogs. However, female hierarchies can create difficulties within the intraspecific relationship, especially when two strong character subjects clash. Another main aspect to take into consideration is the physiological sexual difference. Those who choose a female should know that twice a year she will be in heat: that will not only cause a loss of blood drops (often causing hygiene problem within the household), but also a character alteration with irritability and restlessness. Then, we should always keep in mind the danger of potential unwanted pregnancy. A male, instead, while not being in heat, will be available for mating, all year long. He will respond to the uptake of female pheromones with agitation, disobedience, rowdiness, and attempts to escape in search of a partner. So, during these periods, pets have to be managed with absolute attention and determination. Finally, if you are ready for your first experience, it might be preferable to choose a female, since females of most breeds are easier to train.

How to Choose the Right Puppy

How to know if the young dog, once adult, will have a healthy and balanced temperament in order to integrate itself in the family context and relate normally to the other members of the group?

About forty years ago, William E. Campbell, the American researcher considered as the pioneer of the incipient branch of veterinary medicine then called "dog psychology" (currently maybe more correctly defined as "dog behavioral medicine") developed a structured multi-stage test, on the basis of his multi-year research and experiences in the field. He called it "puppy behavior test."

This real aptitude test represents a hint for breeders and potential pet buyers, and aims at searching for the perfect match between puppies and people, in order to favor a right human and dog coexistence.

Campbell's test last few minutes and should be preferably taken on six-eight weeks old puppies. The first test (social attraction) consists of placing the pet on the ground, taking a few steps back, bending down on knees and clapping hands to call it.

The result, to be note down together with the successive ones on a sheet that will be then

Don't forget that a young dog's behavior is based on its first experiences gained within human environment, rather than from its litter.

analyzed, takes the following answers into account: 1) the puppy came immediately, tail up, jumped on, nipped hands; 2) the puppy came immediately, tail up, scratched hands with paws; 3) the puppy came immediately, tail down; 4) the puppy came hesitantly, tail down; 5) the puppy didn't come at all.

The second test (ability to follow) consists in placing the pet on the ground and stepping away from it. The result falls into one of the following options: 1) the puppy followed immediately, tail up, reached and nipped foot; 2) the puppy followed immediately, tail up, reached foot; 3) the puppy came immediately, tail down; 4) the puppy followed hesitantly, tail down; 5) the puppy didn't follow at all, sat still, took another direction.

The third test (constraint response) consists in placing the pet on the ground, turning it belly-up, and keeping it still for about half a minute. The possible responses are: 1) the puppy struggled and wiggled violently, tried to bite hand; 2) the puppy struggled and wiggled violently; 3) the puppy struggled at first, then calmed down; 4) the puppy didn't struggle, licked hand.

The fourth test (social dominance) consists in

placing the pet on the ground and stroking it slowly
for about half a minute, starting from its head, to
its neck and its back. Here the possible responses:
1) the puppy jumped on, scratched hands with
paws, snarled, tried to bite; 2) the puppy jumped
on, scratched hands with paws; 3) the puppy turned
around, licked hands; 4) the puppy turned belly-up,
licked hands; 5) the puppy walked away.

The fifth and last test (dominance throughout
lifting) consists in placing the animal on the ground,
crossing fingers under its belly and lifting it (about

8 inches [20 cm] high) for about half a minute. Here follow the response: 1) the puppy struggled violently, snarled, tried to bite; 2) the puppy struggled violently; 3) the puppy struggled, then calmed down and licked hands; 3) the puppy didn't struggle, licked hands.

As for the final interpretation, answers 1 reveal a very dominant character (VD); answers 2 dominant (D); answers 3 submissive (S); answers 4 very submissive (VS) and answers 5 inhibited (I). Two or more VD plus D indicate pets with a tendency to react aggressively and bite, if managed abruptly and authoritatively.

Three or more D indicate puppies aiming at standing out rather than being dominated. Three or more S show young dogs that will develop good ability to adapt in any family context. Two or more VS, especially if matched with some I, may lead to an insecure and extremely submissive character, therefore potentially unstable. Two or more I feature dogs that may develop behavioral problem and particular difficulties within socialization. Inconsistent feedback on the results justifies the repetition of the test in a calmer context, however the subjects are probably non-predictable.

Breeds and Pedigrees

Choosing a purebred dog depends not only on personal aesthetic tastes and past experience, but also on the family features the pet will be included in and family members lifestyles.

Not all dogs, for example, are suited to live together with a child, especially if he is few years old or isn't a teenager yet. Among the best breeds, it's worth mentioning the shepherd (German Shepherd, Belgian Shepherd, Scottish Shepherd, Border Collie, Bergamasco Shepherd and so on) mostly provided with an instinctual vocation to care, to be attentive and respectful towards the members of its pack, individually or as a whole and identified as a herd to protect. The Retrievers (Labrador and Golden) are featured by a temperamental balance and strong emotional attachment to human beings, as well.

Those who has a sedentary nature and prefer domestic tranquility to an active life, should opt for the Cavalier King

Charles Spaniel, the Maltese, the Bolognese, the Chihuahua (long life, intelligent and doesn't shed much): they are all quiet and calm, and can be easily carried to keep them close. An equally valid choice is to opt for a large Molosser breed (Bulldog, Cane Corso, Mastiff and so on) or smaller ones (French Bulldog, Pug, Pekingese, Shih-tzu and others): they are all lazy as well as laid back dogs, and don't need too much exercise.

An elderly person may well choose a non excessive size and a quiet temperament dog, like the small and medium size of the Poodle, the Volpino Italiano, the Zwegspitz, the Bichon Frise, the Shih-tzu, the Coton de Tulear and the Cocker Spaniel.

Many breeds are quick, portly and resistant like athletes. These dogs represent the perfect choice for those who love outdoor life, weekends in holiday destination, walks in the woods and sporting life. All hunting dogs (hounds, terriers, dachshunds, cur type dogs, and gun dogs) meet these requirements. Also Terriers and Dachshunds (let's remind that they were born hunting dogs as well) are perfectly suitable for those who like exercise, even if they prefer a smaller size. Finally, let's include Sighthounds (Borzoi, Saluki, Whippet, Galgo and others), and nordic dogs (Siberian Husky, Alaskan Malamute and Samoyed, to mention some of them) that do their very best outdoors, expressing their sporting and playful attitude.

Those who look for a watchdog, should preferably

address to a herding dog. This group ancient progenitor, the Central Asian Shepherd Dog (currently existing and bred in the USA) has always been used to working independently, without particular instructions, committing to the night protection of the herds. All the others descend from it: the Maremma Sheepdog, the Anatolian Shepherd, the Šarplaninac, the Caucasian Shepherd Dog, the Great Pyrenees.

Among the main features of these breeds: ability to work for their owner without him (beyond the strong relationship, this requires great individual decision skills), frugal feeding, resistance to temperature drops, assurance with children, attitude towards resting in daytime and watching at night.

Whatever choice you'll make, dogs would rather be provided with a pedigree, a sort of identification card that not only ensures it's a purebred dog, but also shows its family tree, listing its parents, grandparents and ancestors.

A pedigree is the only official document certifying the subject belonging to a certain breed: to sell a purebred dog without a pedigree can be considered as a fraud. One day, thanks to its pedigree, your puppy will be able to compete in exhibitions, galleries and contests. In case it is used to procreate, its pedigree will enhance the value of its litter. In our country, the leading organization that supervises the registration of puppies with stud books and issues pedigrees is the American Kennel Club (AKC).

The word "pedigree" comes from the French "Pied de Grue", literally meaning "crane foot."

Why this strange etymological reference? It's probably due to ancient manuscripts indicating parentage with some lines traced downwards and forking like tree branches. The drawing recalled the leaving tracks of crane feet. Here comes the French words, then Anglicized as pedigree.

2.
Here Comes the Puppy

Separation from mother, brothers and sisters represents a very critical issue for puppies. They need help to face the experience and overcome it without traumas. Before welcoming your pet home, the environment and essential accessories have to be arranged adequately: the kennel, the food and water bowls, some newspapers sheet and nappies to dirty. During the first days, the kennel may also be made with a cardboard box (you can place soft material inside): better if provided with an opening aside, to resemble a sort of nest, a semi-dark and warm shelter to hide and relax waiting to overcome the initial fears.

Your puppy needs tranquility at first: you should avoid holding it continuously, scaring it with loud noises and cuddling it.

If it weeps, it would be better to ignore it, not to teach it to match the gained attention with vocal calls. Better paying it attention when it's more relaxed. During the first days, it's then important to get it settled and confident with its new home and family members.

Tricks to Get It Used to House Cleaning

It's not difficult to teach your puppy not to dirty the house: you just need to follow some clear-cut rules and be clear in your own minds about respecting some principles. Baby dogs urinate and defecate when their mother stimulates their anogenital region with her tongue, soon after meal: such a behavior stops when they acquire independent sphincter control, generally when they are between three and four weeks old. Later, puppies get rid of liquid and solid excrement without a determined rule: they do it when they feel their urine or feces response. It's nonetheless important to underline that, after their first month of life, most puppies learn instinctively to urinate and defecate far away from meal and resting territorial areas.

So, from their first four weeks of life, it's recommended to start teaching your puppy how to keep the house clean. It's a fact that young, adult and old dogs mostly learn throughout "positive reinforcement": in the long term, a reward after a specific behavior teaches them that they have to behave in a particular way to get a prize.

It's no good rubbing its nose in urines and feces done at home and then spanking your puppy, in order to teach it how to keep the house clean.

In order to teach your puppy how to dirty outside the house, you should first spot the right time, in particular after waking up and after a meal, after drinking and after playing.

In all these occasions, the young dog should be carried to the intended location and so, rewarded (with a stroke, a word of praise or a tasty morsel), better if in the exact moment when it urinates or defecates. To reach the aim more quickly, it may be preferable to walk the dog several times a day, even for few minutes, compatibly with your free time and tasks. Carrying a nappies soaked in urine or dirty with feces and lying it down on the street may lead your pet to recognize the place as suitable to evacuate.

If your puppy doesn't seem to learn, you shouldn't discourage or worst, pick on it: punishment (physical or social whatever) can't help, especially if put into practice when the mischief was done a while before. Instead, you require a great deal of patience, you need to resume the process from its beginning, determined that sooner or later all dogs learn how to keep the house clean.

The Right Diet

When you start feeding your puppy, the greatest doubt is the choice between a home-made meal (fresh food mixed together) and pre-packed foodstuff prepared by specialized companies and available in pet shops. The way puppies grow, their behavior, health, overall well-being and appearance are all closely connected to the nutrition we provide. Home-made food implies individual ingredients to weight according to the doses, cook separately and then mix together in the bowl.

This involves time availability and willingness to devote yourselves to this sort of commitment. It's then essential to buy supplements (as for example vitamins,

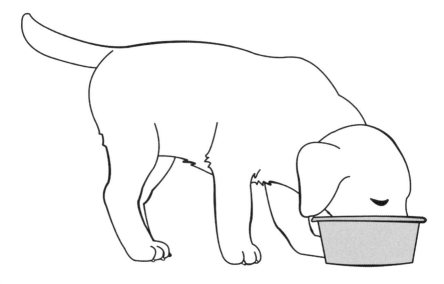

mineral salts, chondroprotective nutrients, etc.) to reach a complete meal in terms of its nutritional value. Most puppies like this solution, though there are those that systematically refuse some of these constituents, discarding them in favor of others. Basic fresh foodstuffs are meat and fish (to cook in boiling water and clean from bones), boiled potatoes or rice (the latter to overcook in order to get a sticky mush), boiled vegetables (preferably carrots, courgettes, green beans, celery, cauliflower, fennel and broccoli), seed oil (preferable to olive oil since it contains arachidonic acid, linoleic acid and linolenic acid) and a complementary based on vitamins and mineral salts. Ricotta, cottage cheese and hard-boiled eggs may occasionally replace meat and fish. Processed food is definitively a more practical and comfortable choice. Such food is already prepared, well balanced and complete. Extra ingredients aren't required.

As for the number of meals per day, there are no fixed rules. Between two and three months old, puppies should eat four meals a day, then three, until they are six months old. From then onwards, you can feed them three times a day or reduce to two. One meal a day is instead definitively not recommended, unlike in the past. The ration should be left available to the dog for about ten minutes and then removed in case it isn't entirely eaten. In this way you can teach your pet not to always have food at disposal, but to exploit the resources when they are available.

First Walks

Contrary to what dog-lovers say, making your puppy stay home until the end of its vaccination course is not recommended. Puppies should gradually get used to outdoor environment: noises, smells, traffic and human beings. It should gradually be trained to all this so to learn how to live a dog's life. Moreover, a puppy should learn to dirty outside, be on a leash, and follow its family on the street. If it grows up cut off from the outside world until the end of its vaccination course (that may last until its four months of life), a sudden exposure to such new experiences may be traumatizing and then affect its psyche as well as its behavior in an extremely negative and irreparable way. It's therefore important to walk it out, paying attention to some aspects: avoid coldest or hottest day time, prevent it from licking everything on the street, keep it away from green areas where mice or rats may have been, beware of unknown and potentially ill dogs. In a nutshell, you should wait before making it live a proper dog's life (including dog play areas): priority should be given to daily frequent but short walks. One of the first teaching is walking on a leash: it can be traditionally attached to collar or – as more and more often – to harness.

Fixed collars (metal, leather, fabric or nylon made) must be put around the neck. The suitable distance between neck and collar is about one finger. Fixed collars main problem is within traction on larynx, trachea and cervical vertebrae, when puppies get the habit of pulling at the leash. Harnesses, instead, allow a more effective control, and dogs can move better than when wearing a collar. Pay close attention: harnesses shouldn't be too tight. They will have to allow your dog freedom of movement without causing problems within shoulder joints – especially in large sized puppies.

Electronic collars or shock collars, which deliver an electrical shock to the neck or the body of a dog, are commonly used as pet containment or bark control system. Despite being forbidden in a number of countries, and regardless of the recent attempts of PETA, the use of these collars is legal in the USA.

Time to Train Your Puppy

It's essential to train your puppy systematically since its early age, in order to get a total obedience from your four-legged friend. Differently than expected, there isn't a suitable age limit for dogs to start learning: each puppy, older than two months, is potentially receptive and well prepared to learn, provided that the exercises are proposed as funny games.

Since when it moves in, it's therefore appropriate to spend some minutes, twice or three times a day, for the lessons, in order to achieve the best results. Simple and basic commands like "Sit!", "Stay!" and "Come!" are essential, that is to say, cement the human-canine bond. Getting a ready response from your four-legged friend is useful to lay the foundation for good education, so to have a much easier to manage pet on your side.

Firstly, it's important to choose a quiet environment, preferably a house room or a fenced garden where puppies don't get distracted. Then, a positive reinforcement is necessary: a treat to give to the student when he answers correctly to what you have asked to do. The positive reinforcement may be a morsel, a stroke or more easily a word of praise: that depends on what works best for your pet. In order to teach the command "Sit!", you should show the dog a reward (like a dog biscuit), then raise it on the top of its head, move it slowly backwards, so that your pet is forced to sit since it monitors the food closely to eat. And that is when you will give the order "Sit!" Immediately after, you should reward it with a treat, repeating the test over and over again, until your dog understands that the command is associated with its sitting and its reward.

After having learned to sit, you can start with the command "Stay!": while the pet is sitting, you should step backwards pronouncing its name and the command "Stay!", and give it the treat when it stay still for a few seconds. Your steps backwards should increase progressively, until you get some meters away. Your dog should sit still and you should almost disappear from sight.

This procedure, as well, has to be taken constantly and gradually. The last basic command is "Come!": once your puppy has learned how to stay still, you can bend on your knees, clap your hands and call it by saying "Come!" When it reaches you, reward it with the usual treat.

First Time Visit to the Vet

The veterinary is fundamental for those who decide to welcome a dog home, as it represents both first-rate reference and a compulsory bridge between the pet and its owner. You shouldn't see the doctor just as someone who will take care of your puppy's health, but also and foremost as a sort of advisor, to make reference to for whatever doubt may arouse within the relationship with your dog. For this reason, it's better to choose a vet as a sole interlocutor to be in touch with during your dog's entire life. In the first visit, the doctor will acknowledge your puppy's state of health, plan nutrition, decide treatment against intestinal parasites, schedule vaccination course and provide

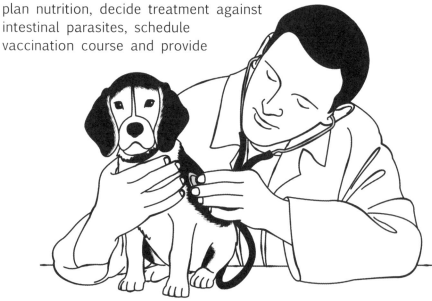

Don't choose your vet just according to logistics, as for example home proximity or low fares.

suggestions on how to establish a proper man-dog relationship. Most puppies are already "parasited" at birth, since their mother transmits them some worms during pregnancy.

Due to placental circulation, the worms reach their body and settle in their intestine. Most common worms are ascarids and hookworms. They may create problems when puppies are about 20-30 days old. Dogs may not show symptoms, but in most cases they have diarrhea, vomit, bad breath, visible presence of parasites inside feces and don't gain bodyweight. So, considering the absolute non-toxicity of the deworming medicinal products available on the market, it's worth carrying out treatment against the worms, even without a preventive feces test.

The treatment, commonly known as "deworming" has to be repeated every 3-4 weeks, twice or three times, according to your vet's instructions. Symptoms like more or less persistent diarrhea, or unshaped and soft feces justify accurate copromicroscopic examinations revealing the presence of intestinal parasites (together with the already mentioned ones) and a more targeted

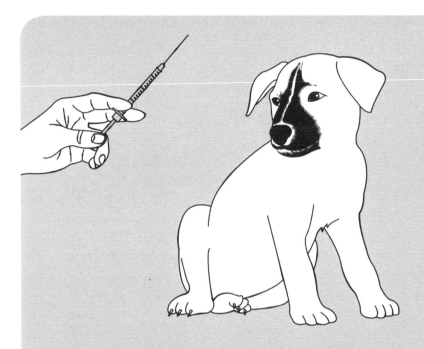

administration of medicines. Vaccination represents
one the most important preventive health care
procedure for puppies. In fact, without vaccinations,
our four-legged friends might catch very serious
and often untreatable infections.

Thanks to immunization, their organism is able
to boost their immune system and adequately face
threats coming from micro-organisms like viruses
and bacteria. That's why one of the first duty for
those who choose a puppy as a friend is to ask
the vet for the vaccination course so to grant
your dog an effective defense against infections.

The first vaccination has to be inoculated
between five and fifteen weeks of life.

There are a few exceptions, though: if you consider that the mother wasn't vaccinated, you should anticipate the beginning of the vaccination course, since your puppy lacks maternal antibodies; the same goes for artificially nursed orphan puppies.

The vaccination course consists of a series of injections, separated by a gap of three weeks. Each injection contains a specific vaccine, that is to say, a biological preparation including micro-organisms (suitably treated not to be harmful) which are responsible for the disease to be prevented: so the pet's immune system produces antibodies which will protect it effectively in case it gets in touch with the same micro-organisms.

Up to three months of their life, it's advisable to submit puppies to the vaccinations protecting your dog from viral diseases (distemper, infective hepatitis, parvavirosis, respiratory disease complex). After that, the young dog's immune system is able to produce antibodies against infections caused by bacteria: vaccinations against leptospirosis should, therefore, be inoculated to more than fifteen week old pets.

The Golden Rules

Choosing a dog as a friend implies duties and responsibilities both towards it and the community we live in. The United States does not require that your pet be identified with a pet microchip, but it is recommended that you microchip it. It is inserted subcutaneously, and thanks to specific readers, a great deal of information can now be obtained: these tiny devices carry 15 figures allowing to detect the birth country of your pet, as well as subject and owner identification (with additional data such as the pet's state of health). The inoculation technique is painless and comparable to a subcutaneous injection with a syringe.

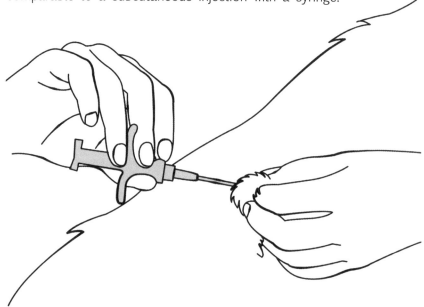

If you register the microchip, your dog's contact information will be accessible at the National Pet Microchip Registration Database, where you can manage your pet's account. More importantly, the microchip is essential when your dog is lost in the neighborhood, as according to a study carried out by the American Veterinary Medical Association, dogs are 2.5 times more likely to be returned to their home if they have a registered microchip.

Anyway, putting a tag to your four-legged friend's collar is a good idea: that will allow anyone to immediately identify the dog's family in case of loss, even without a microchip reader. In the United States, leash laws are different within each State. While some States do not have statewide leash laws and give localities power to make leash law, there are some other States in which leash laws apply statewide. You should always carry bags and scoops for excrement collection and disposal.

According to the highway code, buying ad hoc dog car barriers and safety belts is recommended to those who intend to take their dogs in the car. Finally, don't neglect the importance of an insurance policy. Currently, all insurance companies offer good prices for covering damages done by your dog to third parties (civil liability). Such damages include people and things. The insurance may even cover the costs of diagnosing, treating and managing your dog's illness or injury.

3.
A Dog-friendly House

Furniture based on puppies needs, entirely devoted to them areas, great attention to everything might be risky for their health, and safety: these are some rules to keep in mind when your puppy moves in. Sharing living space and furniture shouldn't be mean allowing puppies to freely use armchairs, beds and sofas.

According to dog language, choosing resting places is up to hierarchically superior individuals: hence, to the owner and then to the family. That's why, since its early age, we should teach our pet to exclusively use one specific area (where to place its kennel and toys). This would prevent its access to furniture and items that it should identify as only belonging to its family, since its members are at the top of the social ladder.

Litters or kennels may well be replaced by mats or cushions: the important thing is to assign your dog a peaceful and stable place where to rest without being disturbed. That should be its own place, a secure area representing its den where to hide when it needs privacy. As for kennels, there are all kinds of models on the market: as always, substance matters more than form, therefore it's important to look for a simple, easily washable and indestructible one.

One more aspect concerning of the kennel: its placement. Many ethologists recommend placing it somewhere out of the way, since constant monitoring of the front door may lead some pets to feel authorized to take a superior social position. In fact, they may feel responsible

Always make the water bowl available for the dog, but get rid of the food one when it's empty and show your dog it full just at feeding time.

for watching who comes and goes. Portable kennels can be used in your own backyard or taken with you when you and your dog travel. They come in various dimensions to accommodate dogs of any size.

As for food and water bowls, it's preferable to choose steel models, both hypoallergenic (plastic ones may be responsible for contact dermatitis) and more difficult to move or overthrow. Some vets suggest placing the bowls a few centimeters, above the ground (sample holders are commercially available) to favor food chewing and drinking, not to force the dog with excess neck stretching. It's recommended to put them in a different place from the kennel area. The kitchen may be a good choice, also because it represents the place where families cook and eat.

Travel bowls are often smaller than kitchen bowls, but they are easier to clean and more compact, so they can be carried.

The Importance
of Playing

The wish and the pleasure of playing (like playful physical, manual or mental activity) stay with us forever, whether we are children, adults, young adults or old. Such a prerogative belongs to the canine species as well, and arises more vividly in pets that live with us sharing life and home.

According to ethologists, playing is not an exclusive activity of young dogs as it implies different motivations and issues. Dogs that play don't only enjoy themselves but also learn to grow up, deal with others, relieve themselves, reduce stress, strengthen bonds of affection, do healthy exercise and so on. A recent scientific research highlights that puppies grown within reduced or absent stimulations and playful activities develop more or less clear behavioral disorders.

Young dogs play with their mother and brothers, learn how to determine their bite intensity, deal with other living beings on a daily basis, imitate adults' behaviors and learn how to behave like dogs for all intents and purposes.

For this reason it's right to state that playing is a proper training ground for puppies. Most adult and old dogs don't lose their will to play: pets make a

To be effective educational means, play time and games should be proposed by the family members, not by the dog. Dogs' requests shouldn't always be accepted.

kind of bow, with their front legs stretched forward and their bottom raised, as a clear invitation to a playful activity. Other times they make themselves understood more clearly by drawing their owner's attention with their barking, their front legs or their muzzle; or by dropping the item they would like to enjoy a bit with, right in front of them.

One of the main aims and meanings of playing is to enjoy: watching our puppy playing is enough to realize why.

Its excited look while it watches our hand ready to throw an object for it to bring back is very eloquent, as well as its happiness when it returns the retrieved ball. And what can we say about dogs frantically chasing each other inside gardens or dog parks? They are undoubtedly a bundle of joy and represent the top of fun.

We shouldn't forget that playing makes our dogs healthy, since it provides them with exercise, strengthens their muscles and keeps their locomotor system in shape. That's particularly true for some breeds which need exercise to increase their body size, during the growing-up process. Boxers, Dobermans, Rottweilers, Labradors and similar need

to shape their powerful muscle mass with exercise, until reaching their final structure.

Playing is also essential within programs of reduction in bodyweight gain (let's remind that overweight and obesity are widespread problems of city dogs), since diet is not always enough to reach the target set. Behavior researchers currently agree that playing represents one of the best dog training techniques.

Playful activities are also part of therapeutic protocols for many behavioral disorders, more and more often found in our four-legged friends. Having fun with our own pet helps strengthen the relationship: playing is a "social glue" increasing chemistry, bonding and mutual understanding.

There are several ways to play with our dogs: among the most well-known ones we should include bringing items back, outdoor chase games, swimming or go jogging together, hiding tasty morsels for our puppy to find, and dog agility.

Buying your dog toys to enjoy and spend good time with is a very effective idea. Such accessories should fulfill some requirements and must not be dangerous as for ingestion, breaking, accidental injuries, intoxication and so on.

Beware of rubber and soft plastic accessories that may be easily destroyed and swallowed. Let's prefer tooth proof, unbreakable, items. Whilst available toys may be of some good help to deceive boredom at lonely times, dog psychologists suggest not leaving your dog with too many "entertainments" available at the same time, but alternating and savoring them, as if they were prizes awarded as a positive reinforcement due to its correct behavior.
Let's remind, then, the importance of our active participation to the game, an activity to promote in our free time, in order to cement and improve the relationship with our four-footed friend.

Dangers in Apartments

Living in apartments turns out to be comfortable, peaceful and beneficial, but may place our pets at risk due to all kinds of domestic situations which should never be neglected. On the other hand, reviewing domestic accidents occurring in our country every year (every year, more than 18,000 individuals in the United States die from home-related accidents), we realize the amount of dangers in apartments and the risk for our pets.

Let's run through items to pay attention to. Ornamental plants potentially toxic to the canine species are: holly, dieffenbachia (elegant white marbled plant), philodendron, ivy, hyacinth, lily, iris, hydrangea, narcissus, oleander, rhododendron, mistletoe and poinsettia.

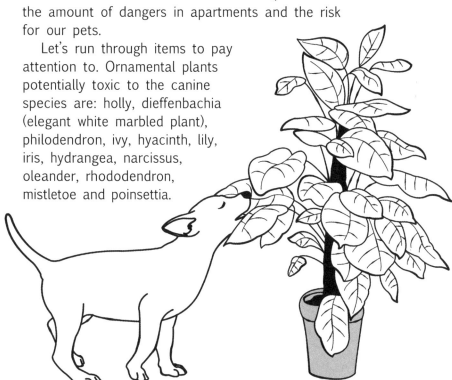

Dogs often express their interest in leaves, flowers, stems and parts of plants in general: they sniff, chew, taste and even drink potholders water. According to researchers, all that mainly arises from their curiosity and, secondly, from their need for fibers as well as from their wish for self-induced vomit to cleanse their organism. Symptoms of ingestion of potentially toxic plants may be: excess salivation, vomit, diarrhea, abdominal pains, difficulty in breathing, impaired heart function, liver or kidney problems, all the way up to neurological disorders, such as failure to coordinate movements, paresis, paralysis, seizures and coma. Those who own a dog should avoid keeping potentially dangerous ornamental plants at home, or would rather place them out of reach, or even adequately protect them with nets or fences. In the case of potentially toxic plants ingestion, a good practice is to try and make your dog vomit within half an hour, force-medicating it orally with water and salt, hot water and lemon or even with some milliliters of peroxide. However, if the accident occurred too long before, it's recommended to get in touch with the vet or the closer poison control center, as soon as possible.

Medicines may represent a quite relevant domestic danger, as well. Many dogs owners believe that human use drugs may easily help their four-legged friend's possible symptoms. Actually, if until about thirty years ago there weren't many other alternatives to human medicines, in the last few years veterinary

pharmaceutical industry has taken a giant step forward, reaching specific molecules synthesis and distribution exclusively intended for dogs. Active ingredients formulated for human species proved to be useless and risky, indeed. Many medicinal products for human use may cause big troubles to pets (symptoms may be, again, varied and multifaceted). A common example is acetylsalicylic acid and so called NSAID, non-steroidal anti-inflammatory drugs. Not to mention that the problem is mostly represented by a wrong dose rather than by the molecule in itself. For all these reasons, do it yourself and self-healing should be avoided. It's instead recommended always to talk to your vet, before delivering a medicine to your dog. The same cannot be said in the case of left unattended medicines which dogs may accidentally swallow. What has been said about ornamental plants also applies to it. Try to make your dog vomit and then, ask the vet or the poison control center.

Prevention is based on the habit of keeping drugs under lock and key, in unreachable places. Within domestic poisoning we should remind many daily products: detergents, soap, antiseptics, insecticides, rat poisons (especially dicoumarol, an active ingredient with an anticoagulant action contained in common rodenticide baits used for rat control), molluscicides, crayons, markers, shoe polish, paint, dyes, mothballs, make up, antifreeze. But the list might be much longer. Pay attention to indirect poisoning as well: if your pet walk on the floor that has just been washed but hasn't already been rinsed or dried it may drink plenty of detergent by licking its paws right after. Don't forget the intoxication caused by inhaled substances (smoke, toxic gases or vapors) or by direct contact (alcohol, ink, fuel etc). Animal curiosity and wish to inspect what surrounds them with their mouth, often lead them to taste non-edible objects, found in their domestic environment, and then swallow them accidentally. At best, all foreign matter is ejected by vomit and feces. However, that's not always the case. The main risk is an intestinal obstruction or sub-obstruction, caused by the object failing to transit in the digestive tract because of the intestinal lumen extraordinary proportions in relation to the foreign matter. In such circumstances, dogs vomit often, may show attempts to defecate, looks wearer and wearer as well as dehydrated. Once the obstruction has been confirmed (throughout blood test, x-ray examination

and ultrasound) the vet should go in surgically.
In case you notice your dog's ingestion, it's essential
to induce it to vomit (see above) within half an hour.

Domestic accidents are also very common.
Doors, shutters and drawers, when slammed even
unintentionally, may cause crush compression of dogs
tails and paws. Smaller size dog may suffer significant
injuries, though. Blinds and shutters have sometimes
proven to be deadly guillotine weapons for pets.
Glasses, knickknacks, and glass objects, occasionally
mistaken for toys or something to chase, may break
or cause injury to your "hunters". One of the most
severe events, is falling from windowsills, balconies
and terraces. That may concern members of the
canine species, as well. Even more or less sneaky
dangers may hide within the home: the kitchen, for
example, is definitely a very interesting area for
dogs, at least for the smells coming from cooking
plates. But be aware of fire and hotplates that are
responsible for paws and muzzle burns.
Smaller size dogs, then, are particularly
sensitive to the gas used to cook and

also to fumes from non stick pans and old fridges freon.

Drowning can also be a serious risk: most pets love water. They can easily drown even in little water, as for example when they attempt to get into the toilet. For this reason, your toilet lid should always be shut. Although many dogs can swim perfectly, swimming pools can also be a real danger for your pet. Also, dogs bring along with them much more stuff than humans, in terms of dog hair and dirt; if you're planning to build a new swimming pool for pets and humans to use, you should always keep the sanitation issue in mind.

Puppies and small size subjects may also be curious of confined spaces recalling a den: for this reason, ovens, washing machines, fridges and dishwashers may prove to be dangerous traps, especially if they are started when the pet is inside. Particular attention should be paid on electrical wires, where electrocution may come from. As for household appliances, it's not only recommended to prevent dogs from getting closer when the electrical goods are activated, but you should also pay attention to electromagnetic waves. As some research has highlighted, electromagnetic waves emitted by electronic devices such as TV sets, mobile phones, personal computers and so on may be a factor for cancer development: such a consideration applies to all living beings (humans included) but it seems to have a bigger impact on smaller body sizes.

4.
Taking Care

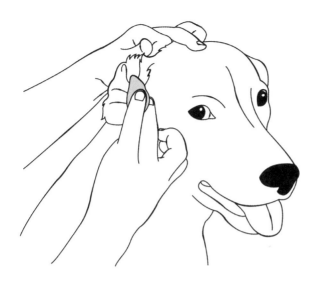

Contrary to common belief, eye and ear cleansing shouldn't be practiced on a regular basis, but only when it's really needed.

After having instilled an appropriate detergent in the canal (drugstores and pet shops sell dogs relevant articles) you can use a cotton-bud or a moist towelette wrapped around your index finger to remove ear wax. Dogs' ear canal is considerably longer than the human one and curves before reaching the tympanic membrane: pushing the stick or your finger deep down doesn't cause any damage.

As for eye cleansing, you may instead use a patch soaked in cooled chamomile (better avoid cotton ones that may unravel). Avoid boric acid solution, since it may crystallize and cause additional local irritation. In the case of abundant lacrimation or semi-solid matter rather than redness, it's advisable to flush the eyes with the patch soaked in chamomile, for a few minutes, morning and evening.

Nail Cutting

Dogs' nails are for digging, scraping rough surfaces and scratching. Our four-legged friends have five nails for their front legs, and four or five for their hind legs whether or not they have their first finger. Such a finger, if devoid of a proper bone articulation, is called spur. Some subjects may also have a double spur. In this case only one of them is structured. If unchecked, dogs' nail may grow abnormally until becoming ingrown (with a following stab in their footpad) or causing walking problems. Walking on tough and rough surfaces (as for example pavements and urban streets) is generally enough to keep your dog's

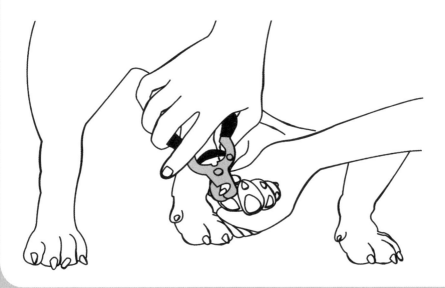

nail short. But beware: its first front and back finger nails don't lay on the ground and don't wear out, so they should be monitored in order to avoid their excessive growth. When required, you can easily cut your dog's nails at home, without necessarily turning to the vet or the groomer: you should bear in mind some important aspects, though, since most dogs detest having their paws handled, and getting them used to nail cutting, when they are very young, is often a good idea. Firstly, it's recommended to equip yourself with an appropriate cutter (available in pet shops). Good quality trimmers should be sharp, concave at the cutting edge and, above all, designed for the correct size of your dog.

Against the light, you can easily notice an internal, conic-shaped and purple structure, featured by a nerve and a blood vessel. Your cut shouldn't affect this area, as it's painful and causes a little bleeding which can be contained with a cotton ball soaked in disinfectant to press on the area for a few minutes. Anyway, it would be a good thing for you to only cut the tip, especially if your dog has dark nails and it's impossible to see it through its internal structures. Nails as well as integumentary system wellness depend on nutrition, as well: a shortage of mineral salts manifests throughout nails fragility and shedding.

Oral Hygiene

Oral hygiene is very important for dogs: taking care of their teeth and gums helps keep such structures healthy and avoids plaque as well as tartar buildup, without following periodontitis problems. However, oral hygiene is often an overlooked factor. According to veterinarians' reports, 85 per cent of dogs over 4 suffer from periodontal disease, a condition that can lead to tooth loss and infection, and which can be avoided with regular dental cleaning.

Good oral hygiene is based on several points: the use of enzymatic paste, toothbrushes, products

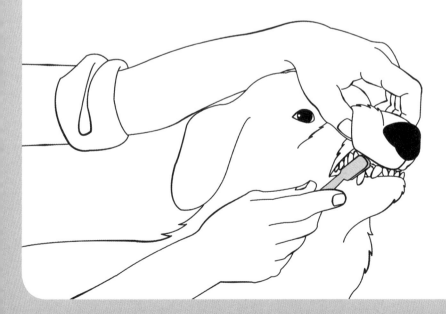

favoring healthy biting exercise and an appropriate diet. Dog toothpaste and enzymatic paste are useful, provided that such products are given on a regular basis. As they are available on the market, the owner's task is easier. Such preparations may be applied locally or mixed together with food to be spread on teeth during food intake. Using a toothbrush is not always practicable but it theoretically represents a very good habit, if only for its mechanical action on plaque accumulating every day. Although pet shop sell dogs tools and kits with plastic caps to place your finger on, a common toothbrush and some patches wrapped around your finger are suited to the task. The important thing is that the procedure is taken on a daily basis, rubbing the point of contact between teeth and gums. However, if your dog can't handle such a tight schedule, just aim to three-four times per week.

Diet is also fundamental for dogs' oral hygiene: provided that rough and dry food favors healthy biting exercise, there are several product lines on the market that can keep your dog's teeth clean, reducing plaque and tartar buildup by about 30 per cent. Such foodstuff action is based both on croquette toughness (forcing the pet to chew) and a mixture of minerals depositing on teeth and helping keep them healthy and clean.

Coat Care

Dogs don't care much about their body, and their habit of spending most of the day outdoors justifies frequent baths; in fact, most of them actually enjoy being covered in smell, mud or dust.

That doesn't mean pets should be washed too often (once every 45-60 days should be enough!) since their sebum protective surface takes long to reshape. Many owners wash their dogs frequently also because of the smell coming from their body. That is, instead, a specific feature of their species, due to some particular integumentary substances. Baths do nothing but increase such peculiarities, as a result of the volatilization of these elements. They develop throughout biochemical reactions that amplify such

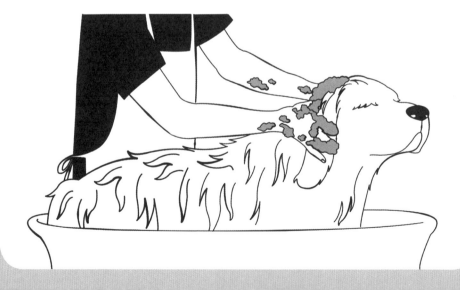

When you wash your dog at home, you should be careful: water or detergent must not enter their eyes, nose, mouth or ears.

odors. That's the reason why, when it rains or your dog gets wet, its coat and its skin smell acrid and intensively. Also, bathing your dog isn't always a joyful and positive experience, as your pet is likely to put up a fight every time you try to get it clean. If you want to wash your dog at home, you'd better use dogs preparations and avoid mild soap for humans or shampoo for children, which are not only unsuitable but can also spoil your four-legged friend's skin. Above all, protect the ears of your pet: you don't want any water to get in there, not only because it is uncomfortable for it, but also because it's something that can actually cause health problems.

In order to monitor dogs' skin and coat hygiene, the most useful care is brushing and combing: such procedures aim at removing dead hair (as well as avoiding it becoming felted and causing dermatological problems), reducing hair dispersal in the domestic environment and minimizing its ingestion during licking, as well as providing the dog with a good looking and tidy aspect. If, under normal circumstances, such operations should be carried out on a daily basis (in some cases even morning and evening), during your dog's molting period, it's better to increase them up

to three-four times a day, especially in subjects with marked molting features. You need specific accessories, even better if recommended by the groomer who is able to understand which tool to use according to your dog's morphology.

Pet shops sell all kinds of suitable kits: different material brushes, longer or shorter toothed combs, slicker brushes, strippers, removing hair gloves and so on. If your dog has long hair, a fine-tooth comb is recommended; if it's rough coated you would rather comb it with a slicker brush; if it has short hair, the best way to treat its coat will be to use a plastic toothed comb. Many dogs don't like being brushed. That's why you should get them used to such a procedure, so that they don't live it like a negative experience. You dog has to be placed on a table, and taught to relax throughout appropriate techniques as well as to keep calm. The brushing procedure will be initially taken for short periods. Then you will gradually increase the time. A positive reinforcement should be matched with combing (as for example a tasty morsel,

a word of praise or a cuddle). That aims at gratifying your pet and makes the procedure pleasant, therefore welcomed. In order to teach our four-legged friend how to relax and stay quiet, a preliminary path is required: leaving it on the floor, you should bend on your knees, or lie next to it, and work on the physical contact. You should get it used to getting touched, trying to tap into pleasant and positive feelings, such as stroking it and massaging it with slow, circular movements on sensitive areas (auricles, hips, belly and lower back from the juncture of its hind limbs); meanwhile, you should talk to it softly, so to match tactile and sound stimuli; once you dog has learned to relax (you can easily understand it from its behavior) you can go through the next step involving the gradual use of brush and comb: the last stage consist in placing your dog on the table and repeating the described preliminary procedures, one after the other. You should bear in mind that each single step has to be carried out with no rush and only when you are sure that your four-legged friend has learned the previous lesson.

5.
Proper
Dog
Training

Living together with a dog often leads to an exasperation of defects and bad habits, since those who choose a dog as a friend empathize with the relationship as if they had to deal with a child.

If on the one hand, a pets' role (after thousands of years spent by men's side), undoubtedly hides positive values, on the other, we must also be aware of an anthropomorphization risk (that is to say a dog's humanization), that implies ascribing typical human feelings and ways of thinking to dogs.

The tendency to humanize dogs dates back to ancient times, just think about Aesop's Fables or more recent Walt Disney films. However, it's appropriate not to exaggerate in this regard, since there is a risk of establishing a relationship based on wrong conditions. It's right to make an effort and live a balanced bond without exceeding severity or indulgence.

Few, but Clear-cut Rules

When you choose a dog as a friend, you first need to keep in mind that it's an animal and must be considered, treated and dealt with as such, recognizing its own role. That shouldn't be negatively or derogatorily interpreted. In fact, animals have very different ways of communicating, rationalizing and acting. Interacting with them as if they were humans involves misinterpretation, indeed. What you can, in good faith, consider as affection and benevolence behaviors, may be interpreted as courtesy and respect by your dog: the result may be an increasing in its dominant social position.

It's recommended to avoid giving in to all its requests, not to revert roles. In fact, it happens quite often that dogs behave like owners (dominant role) and owners like dogs (submissive role). In families

made of several members, a standard line of conduct is required: if someone, for example, allows the dog to lie on couches, while someone else doesn't, the dog won't understand the rules and will behave in a dismissive way.

A useful hint is to establish the so called top dog rule: it consists in following a few suggestions to assign the dog with a stable social position within the family. Following such suggestions, it will be possible to mostly avoid conflicts and problematic behavior. Compliance with the rules is, indeed, strictly connected to a well defined hierarchical role, in canine species. The top dog rule is based on what we see in the natural environment concerning wolves. It consists in: feeding the dog always after family meals (top dogs, after having chased and killed their prey, eat it first, leaving leftovers to their inferiors); teaching it not to pull on the leash, but to always follow he who leads it on the street (top dogs are those who decide where to go in order to comb the area and find resources): keeping it from lying on armchairs, couches or beds, providing it instead with a kennel where to sleep (top dogs choose comfortable places to rest, whereas their inferiors settle in other areas); taking firsthand initiatives, ignoring your pet's requests (whether they are games, cuddles, food and going out, it's important for your dog to understand that decisions are up to you), always proving that you have clear ideas and control of the situation.

Behavior Disorders

The pleasure coming from a relationship with a dog sometimes risks becoming compromised or entirely spoiled when the dog turns out to be a problem for the owner, because of unwanted behavior. Animal behavior alterations have always existed and will probably always exist, but their increase and their following reassessment in a new light, are mainly to relate to wrong establishment-interpretation of the man dog relationship and to a maladaptation of the dog to modern circumstances to which it's daily subjected.

The thousand year old bond linking human beings to canine species, has more and more cemented,

inevitably increasing attention to needs, rights as well as animals physical and psychical well-being. Studying deeply dogs' behavior and disorders, scientists have highlighted a whole series of pathologies.

Most of them come from or are exacerbated by dogs' current lifestyle (now very similar to ours, to some extent), their excess humanization and a wrong approach of the owners to their dogs. Among the most widespread pathologies we should remind sociopaths (in particular dominance syndrome) and mental-behavioral disturbance arising from anxiety factors and stress.

A simple example conveys what may happen on a daily basis: to hush his dog, an owner provides it with food; so the pet learns that, in order to receive its reward, it has to keep barking. The result is therefore the opposite effect to what is desired. Another typical example is about stressed owners: at times of tension, adrenal glands produce a great amount of adrenaline that the dog is able to catch immediately, awakening ancestral hunting instincts it cannot vent anyhow (in fact, the chased prey releases the smell of fear coming from adrenaline growth).

The dog is therefore left with a latent state of dissatisfaction, anxiety and psychical stress. Behavior disorders have to be identified and interpreted as soon as possible. Above all, just ignoring your dog's

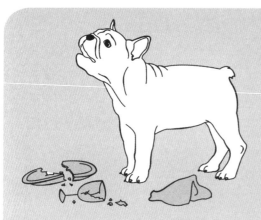

unwanted behavior is plain wrong, because your pet will take such a behavior as acceptable and therefore it can keep it for the future.

Most behavior pathologies tend to get considerably worse as time goes by and make living together with the pet more and more difficult, until leading little responsible people to euthanasia or abandonment.

According to recent research lead by an American team of veterinaries dog behaviorist, the most problematic issues for a dog owner are: aggressiveness (towards humans or other animals), acts of vandalism (destruction of objects or furniture), constant barking (especially at lonely times), inappropriate urination and defecation, phobias, excessive shyness, excessive sexual activity, and digging.

So, where to turn to heal a dog affected by behavioral disorders? The current qualified figure is the veterinary behaviorist: general practitioners aren't

adequately prepared and can't always cope with such situations. Every kind of unwanted behavior can be linked to a number of different causes, including diet, owner's behavior, environmental problems, and excessive stimulation.

Understanding and addressing these causes may prove to be very difficult at first.

Treating behavioral disorders is often a fraught with difficulties road: their solution implies a noteworthy commitment by all the members of the family, together with a significant amount of patience, constancy and goodwill. Behavioral therapy, modification of diet-nutrition and medicines, all contribute to provide good results. Prevention is good as well: at an early stage, puppies should take aptitude tests (as for example Campbell's test described in chapter 1) evaluating dogs behavior features, in view of their possible inclusion within a certain family context, and their compliance with rules of coexistence.

Different Kinds of Aggressiveness

According to statistics, dogs owners mainly complain about their pets' aggressiveness and biting. Sharing one's house and life with an aggressive dog (that may bite you at any moment and must be monitored not to cause damage to people or animals) represents a risk with no doubt. But why some pets are more aggressive than others? Is it always true that a dog becomes aggressive because it hasn't been raised properly or has even been harmed? How can it be that a man is attacked by his dog or a child by its fluffy playmate? Aggressiveness belongs to the canine species ethological background: each subject is potentially aggressive, but that doesn't necessarily mean an aggressive dog is disturbed or behaves in a deviant manner. In some circumstances, canine aggressiveness responds to the application of social

rules, typical of the species. An aggressive dog shouldn't be necessarily branded a bad dog: it can be dangerous, that's true, but this is part of the dogs' way to relate to other living beings, based on their instinct mediated by experience. There's always a more or less valid reason why a dog manifests aggressiveness. If the situation reoccurs and tends to become a problem for those who live with the dog, it's therefore important to identify the source and turn to a veterinary behaviorist. Treatment of behavior disorders – and canine aggressiveness in particular – has recently made considerable progress granting surprising results. The American school of dog behavioral medicine has identified different kinds of aggressiveness. Dominance aggression is mostly common and shown towards members of the same pack for social reasons: dogs are social animals, after all. Territorial aggression is manifested by the dog against strangers to defend its territory, as well as the members of its social group, and all that it considers as its "belongings". The most suitable examples are: the females defending their cubs, the dog attacking the postman, the pet turning to whoever gets close to the car it is inside in a threatening way. Fear aggression (also called pain-induced aggression and nervous aggression) is typical of scared dogs or dogs in difficulty that don't have a chance of escaping and necessarily defend themselves doing it the hard way. A common example is the dog's placed on the veterinary table and undergone

unwelcome manipulation as well as diagnostic treatment,
or the snarling dog attacking he who gets close with
bad intentions and raises his hand to threaten or hit it.
Predatory aggression comes from dogs' never dimmed
ancestral hunting instinct concerning specific subjects.
It leads them to chase and catch running (as if they
were escaping) or screaming sharply preys (such as
cats, small mammals, birds, but also children, cyclists,
and people doing jogging). Some shepherd breeds
activities (biting sheep shines or barking at sheep
to keep them grouped together) have their roots in
predatory aggression, as well, which however has been
"blocked" by training. Intraspecific aggression is, instead,
manifested towards their own kind, as for example
males constantly fighting against other males for mating
dominance. Occasionally, canine aggressiveness doesn't
depend on behavioral factors but on physical problems,
that is to say a proper disease.

Diseases affecting the central nervous system may in fact exist. Their symptoms can be aggressiveness outbursts. A classic example is rabies (an infection caused by a virus well known since ancient times, once called furious rabies), but also some kinds of brain cancer, or infections against encephalon that may be responsible for such a symptom. We should also remind psychiatric pathologies involving aggressiveness and a tendency to bite without a reason: the most well known case is dissociative syndrome (picturesquely called "Jekyll and Hyde disease") a sort of schizophrenia that seems to come from an abnormal kind of epilepsy. When you deal with an unknown and, as far as you know, potentially irritable and aggressive dog, it's a good rule to comply with some basic rules. Firstly, it's advisable to avoid looking directly into the dog's eyes: gazing at it is equivalent to challenge and provoke it. Better look at somewhere else, showing an apparent lack of interest in the dog. Then, it's desirable to assume a non-threatening posture, since men's standing position is higher than dogs' one, so it may be mistaken for an intimidating sign.

Finally, it's fundamental not to provoke the dog and avoid running away, since this would probably lead it to chase you. Also, we must not forget that a dog shouldn't be disturbed, when it's eating or sleeping, not even to stroke it. As for "legally" dangerous dogs, check breed specific laws with your municipal authorities.

Anxious Dogs
and Barking Dogs

Separation anxiety is a pathology due to dogs' hyper attachment to humans and following excessive addiction to their owner. When left alone at home, some dogs panic, "vocalize" all the time, urinate and defecate everywhere, or destroy anything comes their way with teeth and fingernails. Such symptoms represent a way to vent their anxiety and are proofs of a strong state of psychical discomfort that shouldn't be overlooked. Barking is completely natural for dogs: it's a way of

The symptoms of separation anxiety are vocalizations, improper evacuation, and acts of vandalisms coming from dogs' disturbed emotional state.

communication implemented for numberless reasons.

A dog is a proper dog just if it barks. However, constant or excessive barking may turn to be problematic, becoming inconvenient for the pet itself and for the man dog relationship. There are several reasons leading a dog to bark in a maddening way.

Often, such a behavior depends on a wrong educational path. Some dog owners, for example, encourage puppies to bark in order to develop an attitude to guard the territory. Or, a young dog realizes that its whining gains attention so that such a behavior turns into a bad habit at last. To monitor a dog's excess barking you should first understand the reason behind such a behavior. Then you can take steps to address to the problem. In order to avoid suffering solitude and/or excessive barking, the best solution is prevention.

To prevent your dog from moaning when it's alone, you should teach it, in the first place, how to be on its own: firstly for short periods, then, gradually, for longer. For the same reason, you should train it to sleep and stay in its kennel or in its room. Such expedients, will prevent your dog from suffering (therefore from excessive barking) when it's home alone.

Fear of Loud Noises and Improper Evacuation

Dogs' most common phobia is their aversion to loud noises and in particular to storms. This problems may turn into a proper psychosis, throwing them into absolute terror. The most common noises involved in such a phobia are: thunders, firecrackers and gunshots but anxiety may also be related to wheezing, whistling, sirens, machines, household appliances, etc. At times, listening to noises or seeing what causes them, produce dogs' conditioned reflexes: some of them have panic attacks when they see a car or when they hear the sound of its engine. They probably recall a negative experience (an accident, a car hitting, or being taken to an unpleasant place) related to a car. To overcome dogs' fear of noises you would rather apply

hyposensitization and counterconditioning techniques: that means exposing your pet to the stimulus, very softly at first, providing the command "Sit!" and relevant treat, until it learns to tolerate the circumstance without showing anxiety; then, the volume should be progressively turned up, and you should keep working on the basic command and the positive reinforcement. The next step has to be taken only when you are sure your dog has learned the previous lessons. The so called improper evacuation consists, instead, in the excretion of urine and feces in unsuitable places, often in the apartment where the dog lives. Dogs' urination and defecation have a communicative function as well: excrements have pheromones inside and are essential within chemical intraspecific communication. Often, the problem of improper evacuation has an organic explanation (that is to say a pathology affecting the urinary tract or the intestine) but in many cases it's caused by behavioral reasons, as for example dogs' need to mark their territory or a hormonal imbalance. A clinical visit, together with blood, urine and feces tests, will exclude organic reasons. If it's a behavioral problem, together with a specialized veterinary, it's advisable to identify anxiety factors, whether they are stressors or sociopath factors. This will enable to try and remove them throughout a protocol providing behavioral medicine interventions, environmental enrichment interventions, lifestyle changes, or pharmacological changes.

Bad Habits of Biting and Mounting Behavior

For a dog to explore with its mouth is nothing more than its way to learn and understand what is around, also because the sense of touch (which receptors are partly located in the mouth) and taste are fundamental to provide it with detailed information on all it comes in touch with. Puppies' biting and chewing often comes from the discomfort they feel when they change their teeth, but such habits often continue in adults and in old dogs as well. That may be related to playing, but some pets do bite to deceive boredom or because of anxiety and end up ingesting non edible objects (such a disorder is called "pica"). In this respect, it's worth mentioning coprophagia as well, which is a habit of eating feces (considered to be reprehensible by many, but in some way normal for the canine species and not only). In order to discourage the habit of eating their own feces, dogs can be given complementaries which make feces taste disgusting. Mounting behavior may carry different communicative and social values, as well: contrary to common belief, it's not only shown in a sexual context. It represents a playful attitude in young dogs: according to behavioral researchers it's educational, since it will become part of the pet's ethological background. In adult male dogs mounting may be the expression of their sexuality. In more rebel dogs, though, it may represent the attempt to take up a higher social position within its pack. If a male dog tries to mount a human female member of the family (especially if she is going through her period) it might want to acknowledge its top dog right to mate. Also female dogs have mounting behaviors: if they are sterilized, their male component may become evident; if they aren't sterilized, such a behavior should be related to a request (even just of attention) to a human being, or mean a kind of dominance over a subject belonging to its species.

Finally, there is the so called replacement behavior. It may become a ritualized scheme, aroused by an anxiety-inducing component, totally comparable to the one of an introvert child, who, when scolded, relieves himself by sucking his thumb instead of crying. In such circumstances, it's important to deflect your dog's attention distracting it with something playful or involving (throwing it a ball to bring back, showing it the leash for a walk or providing a basic command and relevant treat), so that it can forget what it was doing before and devote itself to something more interesting.

6.
Messages and Senses

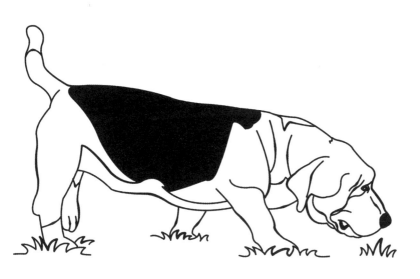

Ethology, the science of animal behavior, clarified that dogs, when relating to living beings, use different kinds of communicative signals: they may provide sound, visual, olfactory, touch and taste information. These ones all refer to the five usual senses. Although there is no interpretive doubt within the intraspecific dog relationship, a misinterpretation of such messages within the intraspecific dog man relationship may happen. As we have already seen, the incorrect interpretation of dogs' communicative messages is often the basis of management and behavior problems. As it's inconceivable for animals to modify their own language in order to get used to their relationship with human beings, it's up to us to try and understand them. Like all living beings, dogs are provided with sensory organs. Thanks to them, our four-legged friends receive information from the external environment, which perception is then processed by their brain. Men have five senses: sight, hearing, touch, smell and taste. But dogs are provided with additional sensory capacities. One – mediated by Jacobson's vomeronasal organ (an anatomical structure placed between nose and palate) – is a middle ground between taste and smell. The other ones – commonly called "sixth sense" (though they would represent the seventh one) – consist of extra-sensory perceptive processes, such as the sense of direction.

Dogs' hearing is considerably developed: they can catch up to 60.000 cycles per second or Hertz sound emission (our ears reach only 20.000 cycles per second). It should also be noted that – unlike human beings – dogs direct their ears (independently of each other) towards the sound source.

Dogs' hearing ability allows them to catch sound waves (ultrasounds) which our ears aren't able to catch (it's no coincidence that ultrasound whistles are used within some educational and training

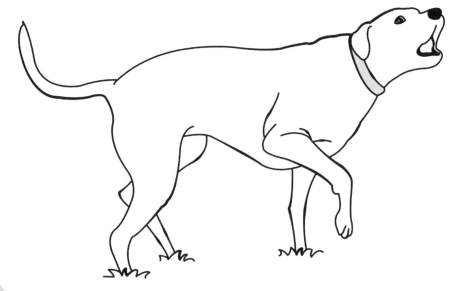

techniques), and provides an increase of their capacity for distinguishing low tones. Dogs can produce significant acoustic messages. Just think of how many verbs identify your dog's vocal sounds: to bark, to woof, to howl, to whine, to whimper, to yelp, to growl, and so on. No other species owns such a rich terminology, to prove how important are dogs' communicative sound signals for us. Each of them means something different to the other ones. In fact, some of these sound emissions have several meanings according to the context in which they are expressed.

Every time dogs emit an acoustic signal, they modulate their voice on the basis of their feelings and of the message they intent to convey. Barking may be associated with strangers, picking up threatening or danger signals, attempt to draw attention, anxiety, happiness, help request, social isolation, perception of different sound stimuli, aggressiveness and so on. A woof is mostly the expression of discomfort and/or physical pain. Yelps and whines are generally laments. They state psychological or physical unease and are intended to stimulate a response by the group. A howl means the presence of some dangers, a request for vocal social contact (as if it was a collective call) or a mating call. A growl is a muffled sound, made with mouth shut. It almost always represents a warning and may anticipate an attack.

Sight and Visual Messages

Sight allows our four-legged friends to catch light stimuli and to turn them into images after having been processed by the brain. Sight represents the main sense in the human species, whereas it doesn't play a decisive role in dogs. Dogs' most relevant anatomical and physiological differences to human beings consist in: three eyelids (upper, lower and third lid or nictitating membrane), lens difficulty focusing and the presence of a "tapetum lucidum": it lies immediately behind the retina and amplifies light stimuli, like a sort of mirror, facilitating sight in bad lighting conditions.

Dogs' eyesight isn't particularly sharp; it can be compared to the one of a slightly shortsighted eye: from afar, dogs can see moving shapes better than us but still figures worse than us. It's difficult, instead, to

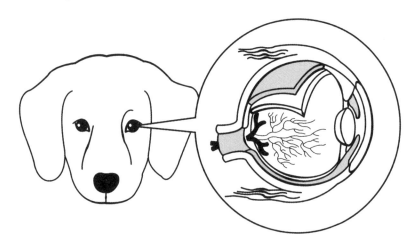

state whether and which colors they are able to catch and distinguish. However, research found out their primitive color vision and their ability to distinguish some of them.

Dogs convey visual messages throughout body postures, expression alterations, or changes of organs as well as of body regions position. Head, ears, eyes, lips, body and tails are particularly important in this respect. By keeping its head raised high, the dog shows confidence and this can also mean hierarchical dominance, in such contexts. Lowering its head, the dog shows insecurity and that may occasionally stands for hierarchical submission. Tilting its head, the dog feels uneasy or doesn't show interest in what is happening around. If the ears are pricked to listen, the dog is careful, sure of itself and in some way wants to prove its own hierarchical dominance. If its ears are lowered, that means the opposite. It shows fear, insecurity and submission. Eyes provide important information on a dog's mood and feelings at a particular time, as well. Miotic pupils (small and narrow) show confidence and tranquility, but also potential aggressiveness. Mydriatic pupils (dilated) denote insecurity and fear. Looking into a dog's eye means a threat and it should be avoided: that's why, if a dog looks into your eyes you had better draw your eye away, as in some cases the dog might attack you. If the dog's look is far away, that can mean a lack of interest or discomfort.

Watching your dog's lips can help you understand its mood. When considering this aspect, let's remind to observe changes (relaxation, curling, emphasis) happening at face folds level, usually accompanied by lip modifications. If its lips are lowered a dog is glad about whoever is in front of it. Lips pulled back are a greeting (as if the dog was laughing). When, instead, the lips are lifted to show gums and teeth, that's a warning that can anticipate a dog's attack.

Together with modification of each individual body region, it's important to pay attention to body postures which dogs communicate their moods through. Pets lowering the front part of their bodies and stretching their front legs, send a clear signal of invitation to play with peaceful intentions. If dogs keel over showing their belly and throat (at times letting out some urine drops), they want to prove their hierarchical submission. When, instead, they raise their hair trying to prove to be bigger than what they really are, they want to look threatening and it's a sign of hierarchical dominance.

The tail is a very important organ for visual communication, as well. If a dog shakes its tail rapidly and joyfully, that means happiness, though some ethologists argue that it's a symptom of discomfort and indecision. A tail down between hind legs and kept still means physical pain but also fear. When the tail is shaken shyly, dogs are insecure and want to show their hierarchical submission. Tail up is an indication of confidence and hierarchical dominance.

Beyond outgoing visual messages, it's important to underline that our four-legged friends (used to relating to their own without the use of words) are very skillful with incoming messages, that is to say with our body language which embodies moods, feelings and emotions. That's the reason why often dogs surprise us. Thanks to their capacity to read and translate apparently meaningless gestures or small changes in our facial expression, they almost seem to read our minds or anticipate our behaviors. Dogs can have empathy for us. They seem to figure out what we are thinking, to communicate with us.

Olfactory and Chemical Messages

Smell allows our four-legged friend to catch the stimuli coming from environmental volatile chemicals and to turn them into odors, after having been processed by their mind. The organ of smell is the nose, in particular the olfactory mucosa (that lines the inside of the nasal cavities), full of specific sensory receptors that send information to the brain, by olfactory nerves. Among pets, dogs are provided with the best olfactory perception: the total surface area of their folded olfactory mucosa is about 18.5 squared inches (120 sq. cm) (the human one is about 0.7 squared inches [5 sq. cm]) and is provided with an amount of olfactory cells between 65 and 225 millions (human olfactory receptors are about 500 thousand). It isn't easy to get into dogs' world and project your

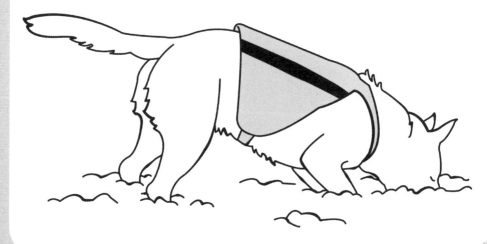

imagination into a reality soaked in smells, in order to understand their perception of reality and their surrounding environment. However it's a fact that thanks to their nose, dogs can also 'see' and 'feel' what's around. Olfactory memory enables them to catalog smells and remember odors. Dogs draw information from smells that human beings aren't even able to imagine. To realize how powerful canine smell is, it's enough to highlight that our friends can recognize acetic acid smell in one drop solution within 1000 liters of water, mixing one drop of such a solution with other 1000 liters of water. If someone leaves his or her fingerprint on a glass surface, a dog is able to acknowledge such a smell even few weeks later. Female dogs are more receptive to smell than male ones, but it seems the males have a better olfactory capacity. Young and old dogs have a less developed smell than adult ones. Dark coated subjects and subjects with pigmented mucosas have a finer smell than their own kind. Behavior researchers almost all agree that chemical olfactory signals represent the most ancient communicative expression within the animal kingdom. Spreading such signals in the environment is for sending different kinds of information, not only to the members of their own species. Within an intraspecific communication, we talk about allomones and kairomones (depending on whether the message benefits he who send it or he who receives it). The words pheromones relates, instead, to an exchange of information among members of the same species. In the latest decades, some scientists have carried out research highlighting that many animal species make use of pheromones: among mammals, mostly carnivores. They are indeed provided with a great number of organic areas where pheromones are produced.

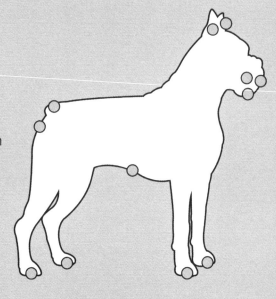

Pheromones are volatile chemicals created by an organism aiming at acting externally, precisely because of their volatility. They are chemical messengers among individuals (the name comes from the Greek "phero" = to bear and "hormone"= "impetus"). They are spread through the air and stay where they are deposited, sending clear and specific information to other members of the same species. There are two fundamental types of pheromones: the first ones arouse an immediate response behavior to the stimulus in those who perceive them (trigger pheromones) and the other ones shape long term physiological modification (priming pheromones) which determine behavioral mutations. The main difference between the two is that the first ones have a purely individual function, whether the other one rule group behavioral response. Dogs catch pheromones by the vomeronasal organ (also called Jacobson's organ), an anatomical structure placed between nose and palate.

Dogs' chemical communication, related to pheromones, has been widely researched and documented. We now know that such substances are for maintaining cohesion inside the group, warning of potential dangers, marking the boundary of the territory, regulating sexual behavior. Many dogs' body parts have been identified as pheromones releasers, though it shall be assumed that there are many other still unknown parts. The following areas are particularly important: the ones full of localized glands between the breasts, the muzzle (lips, cheeks, whiskers, chin), the ears (auricles ceruminous structures), around the anus (which secretion flows into anal sacs), the base of the tail (both upper and lower), the paws (interdigital area and plantar pads). Pherormonal activity substances were also found in amniotic fluid (as well as in saliva, urine and feces) for female dogs to trigger maternal instinct. More specifically, hierarchies would be ruled by the pheromones produced by muzzle, anus and paws glands; social relationships between members of the same pack would be controlled by the pheromones released by the muzzle and paw glands; sexual information would be modulated by the urine and anal glands pheromones.

7.
The Long Circle of Life

Dogs develop sexual maturity within the first year of life. Puberty (hence reproductive ability) is reached between six and twelve months of life, but there are individual breed differences. Generally speaking, large sized dogs cross the finish line later than small sized ones.

Bitches' sexual cycle, that is alternating phases allowing reproduction, recurs every six months and is divided in four different stages: proestrus, oestrus, metoestrus and anoestrus. Proestrus last four-fifteen days during which the vulva looks enlarged, breasts become turgid and blood loss from external genitals occurs. Bitches leave drops everywhere, more or less thoroughly and manifestly. Oestrus, commonly called heat, doesn't last more than four-eight days: this stage corresponds to the fertile period. It matches ovulation and bitches' availability to welcome courtship and mating. In such a phase their blood loss tends to become whiter and watery: it firstly becomes pinkish and then almost transparent.

Metoestrus takes over if pregnancy doesn't occur and lasts about a couple of months. During it, the female reproductive system gradually regresses: the vulva gets back to normal dimensions and aspect, females don't accept male dogs' advances anymore and even tend to push them away in an unequivocally unfriendly way. Anoestrus depends on each subject but on average it lasts a few months: at this stage females experience a physiological rest, during which their reproductive system prepares to the resumption of sexual activity. Although it's said that each bitch is in heat twice a year (every six months), that's not entirely true. Each bitch has her schedules: what matters is that her pace is regular during the years. The same applies to the length of the proper sexual phases (proestrus and oestrus), that should always be featured by the same timescale and the same particular manifestations (changes in external genitals,

entity and color of blood loss, etc.) Bitches in heat look very restless, together with losing blood. When they go for a walk, they mark their territory with urine drops rich in pheromones, aiming at drawing male attention. Their behavior towards possible mates is flirtatious: in fact, they accept males' advances and are willing to mate. In some cases, they may run away to look for a partner. Male dogs, attracted by the female smell, become particularly agitated. At home they aren't very interested in cuddles and food, and spend most of their time by the door to express their wish to go out. Outdoors they're definitively more interested in smells, lick female urine on the street, may try to run away, and start brawling with other males met on their way.

In order to avoid problems about living together, it's recommended to take practical measures. Vulvar blood loss within the domestic environment can be prevented by making your dog wear nappies or pants easily available in pet shops. When you walk your dog in heat, you had better keep them on a leash for them to avoid running away or meeting a mate. Though not all states have leash laws, many of them view animal control as matters of local concern. Before you conclude that there is no leash requirement in your area, call your city or county code office to check your local law. Do not bring a female in heat to a dog park, since fights and scuffles may occur.

Pregnancy: from Mating to Birth

Pregnancy and birth are delicate moments. Therefore, if you really want your dog to deliver puppies, it's advisable to plan all responsibly to avoid problems. The crassest mistake you can make in such circumstances is to let nature take its course, a choice that may start troubles. Among them, increasing abandonment. Therefore if you aren't capable of carefully handling all the phases that lead to puppies birth you'd better give up, choosing instead surgical sterilization. For the same reason, breeding dogs would rather be purebred dogs. Future parents should be chosen carefully, taking into account some important aspects. Firstly, they had better be young: especially bitches that shouldn't be older than seven years, in particular if that's their

first pregnancy. It would be advisable that male dogs are eight or nine years old, as well. Both of them should be healthy, both in physical and psychical terms. In particular, they shouldn't suffer from transmissible diseases, as skeletal dysplasia (elbow, hip, knee), cryptorchidism, hemophilia, epilepsy, etc. Both partners would rather belong to the same breed. When you decide for your dog to mate, it's absolutely necessary to settle puppies in advance. It's advisable that puppies' birth and weaning doesn't coincide with the summer season (when everybody is on vacation), planning the blessed event to occur in autumn or winter. You will have to spread the word among friends and acquaintances in order to find a home to the puppies. Potential adopters should be more than the baby dogs, since often many pull away at the last moment.

Before mating, male and the female dogs should already know each other: therefore it's recommended to bring the two together in a neutral territory, so that they can spend some time together, before the fixed date. When you are sure the two get along well (dogs may have their own, often unjustified, sympathies and antipathies, as well), you can fix the approximate date for mating, according to the bitch's fertile period. During the female oestrus, she should be left alone with the male dog for a few days, better at her place. Dogs' pregnancy last about nine weeks. The most evident changes happen during

the fourth or fifth final weeks: the abdomen grows significantly and continually, the bitch gets hungrier and hungrier, and her breasts become more and more turgid. You don't have to wait until the last weeks of gestation to tell that your bitch is pregnant: for example, in the first two weeks the female nipples turn somewhat "pinker". If you are already feeding your bitch a high quality dog food, a vitamin or a mineral supplement will not be necessary. However, your dog should keep its tone muscle and avoid becoming overweight. For this reason, regular exercise is advised.

There is no progesterone blood or urine test to diagnose pregnancy in dogs. There is, however, a blood test that will detect relaxin, a hormone that is produced in pregnant dogs but is not found in non-pregnant dogs. The tests that provide the most rapid answers are X-rays or ultrasound allowing pregnancy assessment after twenty-twenty-five days since mating. Your vet may ask you to come back at the start of the third trimester (around day forty-five) if he or she wants to take X-rays or an ultrasound of your dog's belly: in such a stage fetuses are clearly visible, as well as their dimension and heart's activity. During the last two weeks of pregnancy, your vet may want to see your pet one final time. Sometimes vets take X-rays during this visit to find out how many puppies are on the way. You'll learn what to expect when your dog is giving birth to her puppies. Knowing how many puppies your dog will deliver is fundamental to live her birth in serenity, without running the risk of having to face difficult situations, unprepared. In some cases, pregnancy doesn't take place after mating: both female and male dogs suffer from sterility, as well. In such circumstances, it's recommended to try again (possibly with other partners) to determine who is responsible for the failure. There may be embryonic reabsorption or abortions, as well, They are quite common in dogs. The main cause are: stress (psychical or physical), infectious diseases (a vaccine against herpes virus is available), different kinds of traumas and pharmacological treatments.

During the whole pregnancy, the bitch should lead a quiet life, and you should acknowledge abnormal symptoms (such as vulvar loss, lack of appetite, a decrease in liveliness and so on) as well as carry out relevant checks. When faced with unwanted mating or pregnancy, it's important to promptly terminate the pregnancy with specific pharmacological treatment or a surgical procedure.

Birth and Parental Care

In most cases birth takes place spontaneously with no problems whatsoever, following the natural course of the events. However, it's advisable to plan everything accurately, in order to avoid any kind of trouble.

During the days before birth term, the mommy-to-be may look more nervous and agitated than usual. She may constantly look for her family's attention trying to prepare a sort of den somewhere discreet (whereby she piles up collected soft material) or scratching the floor with her paws. Another warning sign is her sudden lack of appetite: some bitches stop eating showing no interest in food whatsoever. When birth is near, it's good

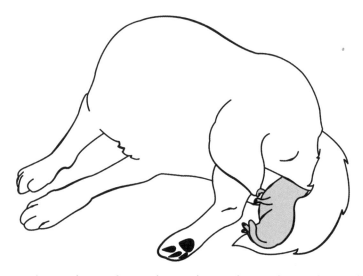

When pregnancy is coming to an end, it's advisable to take note of 24-hour veterinary centers telephone numbers as they may be useful to contact.

to start measuring the bitch's body temperature, morning and evening: after having placed the thermometer in the pet's rectus, you will have to read the temperature and jot it down on a notebook. Close to birth, rectal temperature goes down by about one grade (usually 38-39 °C [100-102 °F] but it's important to take individual data into account, as well and daily fluctuations and changes occurring day by day. In case, you had better call the veterinary so that he or she's ready in case of emergency. When birth occurs with no problems, labor mainly starts at night, due to neurohormonal reasons. The dilated phase (when the vagina dilates) is followed by the expulsive stage, when she delivers baby dogs one after the other. The gap between each single birth may vary and lasts up to twenty four hours. Is essential to stay with your dog when labor begins, in order to provide her with your support and check the situation: in some cases, problems may occur and she may need your help. Call the vet if the pet looks agitated, breathes heavily, has got no place to go, moans, often changes position, is restless, suffers from tremors, pushes insistently without delivering puppies, has strange blood loss. Special attention should be paid to "water breaking" (the rupture of the amniotic sac) that must be followed by the expulsion of the puppies within not more than one hour. It may happen that something goes wrong with the births sequence: a spontaneous birth doesn't necessarily end all safely. That's why it's important to follow your pet from beginning to end, checking that the number of the puppies corresponds to what expected. In case of problems, the vet's early intervention is crucial. He or she can help the bitch deliver throughout manual, pharmacological or surgical (c-section) procedures, as appropriate and according to need. In about ninety-nine percent of the cases, your pet will provide for her offspring by herself: at birth, she breaks fetal sacs to facilitate puppies' release, eats the placentas, licks her puppy dogs to clean them, encourage them at breathing and help them feed. Within 24-48 hours after birth, the mother takes care of

her puppies all the time, leaving them alone just to eat, drink and relieve herself. She often walks away from her den just to dirty, since the intake of placenta supplies her with adequate energy, proteins and water. The most common breeding problems occurring during the days following birth are: lack of maternal instinct and shortage of milk, two often insoluble disorders, which have to be dealt with artificial milk replacement.

Mastitis, an infection of the mammary glands, is another common problem and sometimes it can be difficult to find out. In fact, if localized in one gland only, the bitch will show no sign of illness. This is why the milk coming from each gland should be checked daily as for color and consistency.

Anyhow, puppies should intake colostrum, that is milk produced by the mammary glands during the first days before birth. It is rich in antibodies so that puppies can defend themselves from bacteria and other micro-organisms carrying diseases.

8.
Make
It
Always
Feel
Well

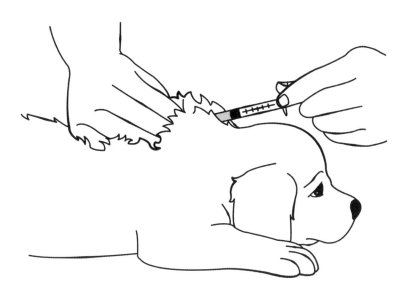

Today more than ever, health checks for dogs are mostly based on the so called preventive medicine, as in the human field. Its main points are: regular dog vaccinations, anti-parasite treatment, regular vet visits, adequate diet, healthy lifestyle and surgical sterilization (in cases where it is required). After the first vaccination course, it's advisable to provide your dog with regular, annual vaccinations. A vaccine is a laboratory biological preparation made by killing or weakening a disease-causing micro-organism which the pet has to be protected from. Vaccines are now being divided into two classes. 'Core' vaccines for dogs are those that should be given to every dog. 'Noncore' vaccines are recommended only for certain dogs. Whether to vaccinate with noncore vaccines or not depends upon a number of things including the age, breed, and health status of dogs, the potential exposure of the dog to an animal that has the disease, the type of vaccine and how common the disease is in the geographical area where the dog lives or may visit.

The core vaccines for dogs include distemper, canine adenovirus-2 (hepatitis and respiratory disease), canine parvovirus-2, and rabies (recommended for aggressive dogs and pets that come into contact with wildlife). Noncore vaccines include leptospirosis, coronavirus, canine parainfluenza and *Bordetella bronchiseptica* (both are causes of 'kennel cough'), *Borrelia burgdorferi* (causes Lyme Disease). Consult with your veterinarian to select the proper vaccines for your dog. If you take your pet from the United States to a foreign country, work with your vet in order to find out what tests, vaccinations, paperwork, or inspections are required by your destination country and when they must be completed. Protecting your pet from parasites is another important way to safeguard its health. But not only: the modern perception of man dog relationship implies living closely together. That means sharing house spaces as well as beds, couches

and armchairs. On that basis, and taking into account that many parasite agents can also attack human beings, prevention protects human wellness as well as our houses against unwelcome guests. Prevention procedures against fleas, ticks, mites, intestinal worms and so on should be taken on a regular basis and should be carried out after having consulted with the vet, avoiding doing-it-yourself. Fleas are tiny, visible to the unaided eye insects: they are laterally flat shaped, a few millimeters long, dark colored and provided with three thick legs. Thanks to them they can jump a distance of about thirty centimeters. They feed on their host's blood and perfectly adapt to live on the body of several species. Fleas cause your pet problems such as: bloodletting, itching caused by bites (that leads dogs to scratch insistently), skin allergic condition (due to a substance in their saliva) and the transmission of the *Dipylidium caninum* parasite (a flat worm settling in dogs' intestine). Ticks are ectoparasites as well. They act pathogenically, affecting several animal species, including human beings. They suck blood, are round shaped (similar to lentils) and well visible to the unaided eye (between a few millimeters and one centimeter long). When ticks embed in the host's skin, a mechanical phase of penetration takes place, followed by an anchorage favored by saliva glue substances ensuring a secure, firm grip. Ticks danger is not so much their blood sucking, but their inoculating pathogenic micro-organisms that may cause infections. Some of them can be severe, such as piroplasmosis, ehrlichiosis, anaplasmosis, borelliosis and rickettsiosis.

Intestinal Parasites

Intestinal parasites are commonly found in dogs' intestine. Such unwelcome guests may be sometimes transmitted to humans. Infected dogs contaminate their surroundings by passing eggs in feces. People can acquire parasite infections by coming into contact with an environment contaminated with eggs. Intestinal parasites are divided in Protozoa, Nematodes (roundworms) and Cestodes (tapeworms). Protozoa are one-cell organisms (therefore microscopic) and are found in soil, ponds and humid environments. The most important are Coccidia and Giardia. Coccidial infections cause hemorrhagic diarrhea and mostly infect puppies. Giardia is an up-and-coming parasite which doesn't always show conspicuous clinical signs and may be transmitted to humans as well as to other cohabiting animals. Therefore, avoiding direct contact with dogs' feces is essential. Ascaridis, Hookworms and Whipworms are roundworms. The first two (that may affect humans, especially children, with larva migrans) are well visible in feces and are common in puppies, which are born already parasitized. Whipworms are instead typical of adult dogs. They take whipworms orally, as a result of an intake of infective feces of their own kind. Such infections, though showing diarrhea, dehydration, vomit and growth anomaly, are mostly asymptomatic. Tapeworms, instead, belong to the Cestodes classification.

The most important dog tapeworms are: *Dipylidium caninum* and *Echinococcus granulosus*. The first one, also called flea tapeworm, double-pore tapeworm, or cucumber tapeworm, infects organisms afflicted with fleas and lice. Dogs' accidental ingestion of insects, in the attempt of scratching themselves with teeth, favors the development of the immature form inside dogs' intestine. Such a tapeworm (that may occasionally affect humans, as well) is asymptomatic, but you may often get aware of its presence by recovering proglottides (tail segments similar to melon seeds) in your dog's feces, around its anus or in its resting places. *Echinococcus* has more to do with the development of large, potentially fatal cysts (mainly lung and liver ones), caused to humans and other animal species (bovine, porcine, ovine and caprine animals) by Cestodes immature forms. The parasite is spread by dogs ingesting infected herbivores' raw viscera. *Echinococcus* is an important world-wide zoonoses, currently wide spread in third countries, in particular Central and South America, Africa and some Asian regions.

Heartworm Disease

Heartworm disease is a serious parasitic disease. It is caused by one foot-long worms (heartworms) that settle in dogs' heart. It is spread through the bites of mosquitoes and causes a kind of cardiac disease. Signs of heartworm disease may include cough, reluctance to exercise, fatigue after moderate activity, difficulty in breathing. Without prompt surgical removal of the heartworm blockage, few dogs survive.

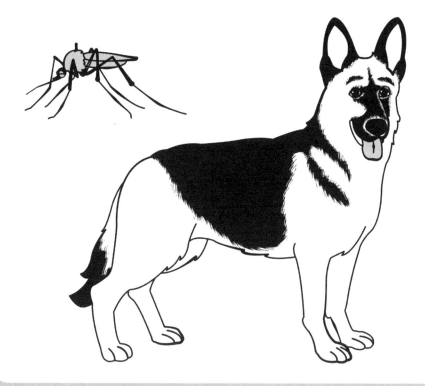

Mosquitoes play an essential role in the heartworm life cycle. They inoculate dogs' body with microscopic baby worms called microfilaria that circulate in the bloodstream, until they reach the heart. Once inside a new host, it takes approximately six months for the larvae to mature into adult heartworms responsible for the disease. The heart localized microfilaria produce new baby worms that enter the bloodstream and can be ingested by mosquitos when they feed on blood. So, the cycle starts again. Although at one time confined to the southern United States, heartworm has now spread to nearly all locations where its vector, the mosquito, is found. Transmission of the parasite occurs in all of the United States. The highest infection rates are found within one hundred-fifty miles of the coast from Texas to New Jersey, and along the Mississippi River and its major tributaries. Heartworm prevention is bases on the intake of specific drugs (administered by the veterinary) during seasonal transmission periods. Starting from the arrival of mosquitoes, monthly treatment lasts until the beginning of winter, when the insects disappear. In regions where the temperature is consistently above 57 °F (14 °C) year-round, a continuous prevention schedule is recommended. A twelve months sustained-release injection is also available for those who may forget monthly procedures. Heartworm symptoms may occur even after a few years since contagion. Annual heartworm testing is necessary, even when dogs are on heartworm prevention year-round.

Leishmaniasis

Leishmaniasis began appearing in North America in 1999 and, as of 2008, Leishmania-positive foxhounds have been reported in twenty-two States. However, due to a lack of surveillance, the disease may have been present in America even before the 1999 outbreak. According to research, such pathology is now endemic in the USA foxhound population. Although leishmaniasis is a zoonotic disease (an infectious disease of animals that can be transmitted to humans) the contagion is never transmitted by an ill organism to a healthy one: the intervention of an intermediary transporter is required (sandflies). Luckily for us, but unfortunately for dogs, the pathogenic agent

prefer our four-legged friends' organism rather than humans' one. Such a disease, doesn't always appear manifestly: especially in the first stages, it's almost asymptomatic. Dogs may incur general unwellness, a shortage of appetite and liveliness, thinning, lymp nodes growth and a weakened state. Clinical signs often affect integumentary system: itching is responsible for different kinds of dermatological injuries mostly followed by auricle ulcerations, dandruff and an abnormal nails growth. Among the mentioned symptoms chronic diarrhea, eyes alteration, lameness and walking difficulties, nose bleedings and neurological disorders. Since leishamaniasis vectors are sandflies, the disease can be partly prevented by using insecticide, nets, preparations (natural and non natural) that keep flies away. It's advisable to avoid walking your dog during the sandfly season from dusk to dawn. Leishmania vaccine appears currently to be the most effective and promising vaccine for dogs. The vaccine is currently available commercially in Brazil and Europe. Treatment options are also available in the USA, but unfortunately none of these treatments lead to life-long sterile cure. The future for Canine Leishmanias control should be an effective canine vaccine and the use of long-acting topical insecticide applications. A vaccine would prevent the establishment of infection introduced by the bites of those sandflies that escape the insecticide effect.

How to Know if It's Sick

As for humans, dogs happen to be indisposed and get sick, as well. Sometimes they need medical checks or prophylactic treatment to counter the risk of diseases. An apparently healthy dog should visit the vet at least once a year (but more often if your dog is older than seven years or has special medical needs). That also depends on the geographical areas where it lives and its

Dogs are not so different from us, and when they don't feel well they send us messages similar to the ones we send when we feel sick. What matters is getting these messages.

epidemiological risks. The vet will have to assess its state of health as regards vaccinations, parasites, dental care, nutrition, exercise. Diagnostic tests, surgeries and specific surveys are required in the case of diseases. Knowing your dog day by day and interpreting its behavior is absolutely helpful to spot sickness, feeling unwell or diseases. A basic piece of advice is observing it carefully on a daily basis. Behavioral changes can also be one of the first signs that your pet is not well. The signals that must make you suspicious are: a lack of appetite and liveliness, laziness, abnormal feces, food or foaming excretion, sneezing, cough, excessive itching, a tendency to frequently shake the head and scratch auricles, excessive thirst, walking problems, excessive lacrimation, production of sticky matter in the inner corner of the eyes. The gums of your pet should always be pink, and its nose moisty and cool. If this occurs suddenly and don't pass on its own within a day or two, tell your doctor and ask advice. As it's the case with human beings, looking for advice on the Internet might seem a good idea, but in several circumstances it is not. Always ask your vet for advice.

Diagnostic Tests

In human medicine, diagnostic tests (medical tests performed to aid in the diagnosis or detection of disease, injury or any other medical condition) have recently gained increasing importance, until becoming fundamental tools to reveal medical conditions in advance (even before symptoms occur).

The same applies to dogs. The progress made by veterinary medicine allows routine blood and urine tests, X-rays, ultrasounds, doppler ultrasounds, cytology, histopathology, endoscopy, CT scans

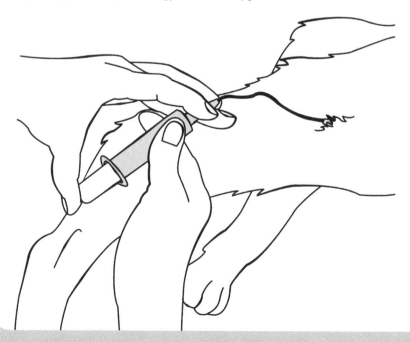

and magnetic resonance. Some of these tests are pretty sophisticated and require specialist equipment, whereas others are easily available in any veterinary unit. The average adult dog annual wellness examinations are the norm, and for middle aged or geriatric dogs semi-annual examinations are recommended. Such examinations include blood, urine and feces tests. Blood would preferably require fasting. If possible, don't feed your pet for about six hours before your appointment. Generally speaking, the test provides the results of a complete blood count, albumin, alkaline phosphatase, alt, amylase, bile acids, bilirubin, bun, calcium, cholesterol, creatinine, ck, glucose, phosphorus, potassium, sodium and total protein.

A urine sample can provide information about several organ systems. Urine may by collected in any sort of clean container (if necessary with the help of a syringe without needle). Preventing your pet from urinating prior to the appointment will assure that your pet's bladder will contain urine for sampling. The test provides diagnostic information concerning physical and chemical properties, acidity or alkalinity, presence of particular substances and evaluation of cell elements.

As for feces, a small sample is enough. Microscopic examination can confirm or exclude the presence of parasites.

Surgical Sterilization: when Needed

Neutering pets is highly promoted and performed in a large majority of animals in the United States, but rare or at least not common in many European countries. Surgical sterilization has a number of beneficial effects on the animal's health, and from the viewpoint of most owners, on the animal's behavior: in other words, sterilized animals, in general, make more desirable family members.

Then, surgical sterilization curbs pet overpopulation. By letting nature take its course, a bitch would deliver an average of six puppies at least once in her life (let's say three males and three females).

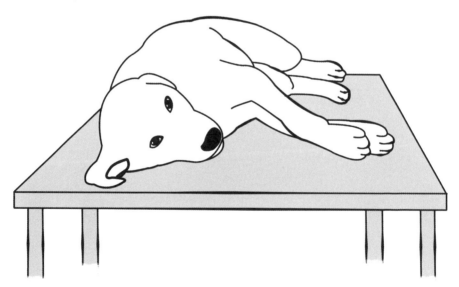

Surgical sterilization makes dogs more suitable to domestic coexistence. It reduces the stray dogs problem as well as reproductive system diseases.

In turn, the three female dogs would deliver other eighteen puppies, within a couple of years at most. After twenty-four months the dogs would amount to fifty-four.

If mathematics is not an opinion, within the next five years the puppies looking for a family would be slightly less than seven hundred, leading to increasingly complex calculations and more and more severe management problems.

To make a long story short, within ten years the number of the pets would have multiplied to five hundredfold, without considering that under normal conditions there would be a birth every six months, so that figures would rise at an exponential rate. This four-legged 'army' would need to find a home, with the risk of exacerbating the already complex question of stray dogs.

Finally, it's worth thinking that there is no dogs' menopause. That means, they are fertile and sexually active throughout their entire life.

However, the hormones produced by their organism may dangerously affect their reproductive system, causing different kinds of pathological problems.

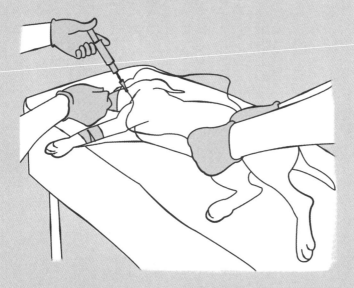

Surgical sterilization has many practical advantages, therefore. But what is exactly surgical sterilization?

Also called gonadectomy, it consists in the removing both gonads ("neutering" or castration) in males; in females, the uterus is removed in concert with both ovaries ("spaying" or ovariohysterectomy). It's a proper surgical procedure and is performed under general anesthesia.

The more and more effective and safe narcotics availability, well-established surgical techniques as well as professional and well prepared veterinaries spread all over the country, make gonadectomy a routine procedure mainly without risks. Post-operative period lasts approximately seven to ten days and requires appropriate antibiotic therapy.

You should check wound healing progress and

caution should be exercised in daily life until the wound is fully healed. Surgical sutures removal concludes the post-operative stage. Then your pet can easily go back to its old life.

As for owners skepticism about psychological repercussions that may affect their pet after the surgery, it's important to underline that animals aren't able to understand that they have been deprived of their own masculinity or femininity.

This is typical human heritage and guilt. Sterilization doesn't change dogs' behavior: at most, they will be quieter and happier to fondly interact with their owners. As already said, gonadectomy has beneficial effects on dogs' behavior.

Another concern commonly expressed by owners is that spaying or castrating their pet will cause it to put on weight, and indeed, gonadectomy appears to be a risk factor for development of obesity. To avoid such a physiological phenomenon, subjects that don't do exercise and exclusively enjoy food and sleeping should be recommended a dietary regimen which takes case-by-case caloric intake into account. Better if combined with daily exercise.

Third Age: Main Health Problems

As in humans, dogs' life can be divided in periods: aging stage generally begins after 6-8 years of life (its process is mostly inversely proportional to dogs' size), whereas proper aging starts before 9-11 years of life. Dogs lifespan has recently been increasing, as well as humans', mainly due to their change in lifestyle, veterinary medicine progress, and owners' paying full attention to the needs of their four-legged friends. During dogs' third age, typical modifications occur, as for example, the impairment of some organs and systems. The liver may encounter problems in storing food resources and eliminating the accumulation of substances. The bowel becomes

sluggish: the traveling food may easily cause symptoms such as constipation or diarrhea, due to reduced tone of the intestinal muscle. The kidney may encounter chronic degenerating that prevent the proper disposal of nitrogenous waste. The skeleton becomes more fragile; it may not carry out adequate support function, due to excessive bone resorption. The heart activity may become insufficient and cause an inadequate blood flow. The immune system weakens and may lead to infections and diseases. Dogs may turn to be less responsive to external stimuli and therefore have their reflexes dulled. Teeth cover in tartar, may become less stable (with the risk of falling out) and the mouth produces bad breath. Old dogs may suffer from a stiff or unsteady gait, with difficulty in walking, especially when climbing or coming down the stairs. Coat hair, especially muzzle ones, may go grey, making dogs look old. Optic lens undergoes a gradual process of opacification (called senile cataract) impeding clear vision. Hearing becomes less sharp leading to more or less clear deafness. There are also psychical changes: older dogs do less physical exercise and change their sleep patterns: they tend to sleep more, for shorter periods and less soundly. Mood swings occur on a daily basis, making dogs irritable or excessively quiet. They may feel disoriented, even at home, at times. Human interaction may decrease. Dogs may not look for attention or physical contact and they may not

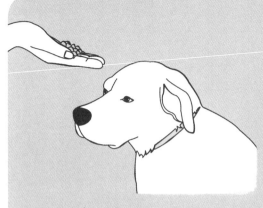

greet their family members. Regression may occur, as for example an increase in oral exploration or the tendency to urinate and defecate in unsuitable places. Some subjects may become anxious and show symptoms such as hypervocalization or a desperate search for their owner who they don't want to separate from. For all the reasons above mentioned, old dogs may incur in health problems more easily than in other stages of their life. Age-related behavior issues, such as cognitive dysfunction, destruction behavior, restlessness (including waking at night) are also common. Compulsive behavior, that is a repetitive and pointless habit, may be the case when your dog keeps licking itself in the same spot, tail chasing or staring at walls or shadows. Aggressive behavior towards humans may occur when the senior dog is subject to drastic changes in the family's composition, following to divorce, death or birth. Also, if a new pet is introduced in the family it can undergo aggression by the older dog's part.

Heart valves pathologies are pretty common during

dogs' third age. Also called endocardiosis, it mainly affects small or medium sized dogs. It consists in a non perfect closing of one valve regulating blood flow throughout the chambers of the heart. This is due to factors of a degenerative kind. The consequence may be a sort of congestive heart failure, which symptoms are cough (especially at night), fatigue after even small exercise, difficulty in breathing. X-rays, echocardiographies and electrocardiographies are required to identify and clearly define the problem. If promptly carried out, specific therapies throughout dogs' entire life ensure a good quality of life. Arthrosis is pretty common in the third age and may affect all dog sizes. The pain is manifested by more or less significant limping which leads to immobility in the most serious cases. In order to face such a pathology, veterinary medicine research has developed both preparations that strengthen joint cartilages and extremely effective and well tolerated anti-inflammatory drugs. Though such treatment doesn't solve the problem permanently, its long-term administration helps the pet with its reduced mobility, ensuring an extension of lifetime under more than acceptable conditions.

Thickened foot pads and brittle nails can also cause problems to your dog's mobility. Together with impaired mobility, senses may become impaired as well. For example, your pet's sense of taste might decrease due to problems in taste buds' sensitivity.

Cataract is almost inevitable in more than seven to nine year old dogs. It's an opacity of the lens process leading to eye "veiling" and gradual loss of vision. In the most serious cases, pets becomes totally blind. Sophisticated surgical techniques, as phacoemulsification. (in which the eye's internal lens is emulsified with an ultrasonic handpiece and aspirated from the eye) ensures sight recovery within short time. Chronic renal impairment is common, as well. It arouses from a degenerative process and causes a gradual loss of kidney filtration ability. The main symptom is thirst, followed by abundant urination. The disease development is featured by decreased appetite, vomit, thinning and a progressive weakened state. Early diagnosis, carried out by blood and urine tests, allows to take measures throughout a specific treatment based on fluid therapy, diet modification and specific drug administration. All this will delay the damage progress and provide dogs with a better quality of life, over a longer

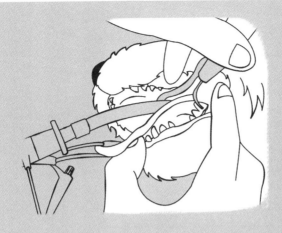

period of time. Dental diseases are widespread in older dogs. Bacterial plaque turns into tartar with following inflammation, lack of stability (tooth loss), and the risk of spreading the infection in other parts of the body, throughout blood flow. So, the mouth produces bad breath and dogs encounter problems or feel pain when they eat their meals. The treatment involves a total teeth cleaning (scaling) carried out under general anesthesia – and possible extraction of decayed teeth – followed by a short course of oral antibiotics. Dogs' tumoral pathologies have definitively increased in the last few decades. However such diseases don't affect just older dogs, it's easier to be seen during their third age. All organs and systems may be affected by cancer which is often asymptomatic. Dogs' owners should get suspicious if the following symptoms occur: external swelling, lack of appetite, thinning, bleeding, trivial matters tending not to heal within a short time.

How to Make Old Age Happy

What are the major suggestions when your faithful friend stands on the threshold of the third age? Firstly, it's advisable to change its diet, as it may gain weight.

Meat and cereal rations should decrease, whereas vegetables should increase. Dogs may also need more water as they age.

Let's remind that seed oil (a teaspoon per five kilograms of pet weight), vitamins and mineral salts would rather be added.

Alternatively, prepackaged food for older dogs is available on the market. Among them, specific meals prepared according to advanced research, aim at counteracting cerebral aging and related to age behaviors.

Some senior dogs might suffer from arthritis, and their diet should keep this into account. Lack of appetite is also common, as disinterest in food grows together with age.

Then, dogs should undergo accurate medical examinations twice a year.Blood tests, X-rays, electrocardiogram and ultrasound help investigate unclear or suspicious clinical signs.

Lifestyle is fundamental to provide dogs with happy old age, as well. Dogs should do daily exercise, without exaggeration and avoiding short as well as intensive efforts.

Families would rather try and involve their dogs in family life, engaging them in activities that keep their mind elastic and agile. Drugs and anti age supplements may turn to be fundamental for old dogs' mind and body wellness.

Recently, veterinary medicine has developed particular molecules (as for example cerebral vasodilators and mood stabilizers) that slow the aging process helping pets to stay responsive and present. Such drugs should be only administered by your vet.

As for nutraceuticals (on general sale but always to be purchased on vet's advice), they are a mixture of antioxidants and anti-inflammatory natural molecules that slow the aging process and counteracts the action of free radicals.

PIERO BIANCHI graduated in medicine veterinary at the University of Milan and he has always devoted himself to the care of pets. Now he works as a professional veterinary in his own clinic in Milan. He specialized in internal medicine and works with dogs, cats and small mammals. He is a publicist, as well, cooperating with Italian magazines and TV-radio stations. He has also published several books (mini encyclopedias, handbooks and collections of stories).

MARISA VESTITA studied painting at the Academy of Fine Arts of Lecce and at the same time she did internships in comics, stage design and stage-craft. Always curious about everything regarding the world of images, in 2002 she moved to Milan where she received her first commissions as an illustrator. She is very interested in applying computer technology to art and completed a course in digital graphic design at the IED (European Institute of Design). She shows in major exhibitions throughout Italy. To date, she collaborated with major Italian publishing houses and magazines, including White Star Kids.

WHITE STAR PUBLISHERS

WS White Star Publishers® is a registered trademark property of De Agostini Libri S.p.A.

© 2016 De Agostini Libri S.p.A.

Via G. da Verrazano, 15 - 28100 Novara, Italy - www.whitestar.it - www.deagostini.it

Translation: Contextus Srl, Pavia, Italy (Vittoria Farallo)

ISBN 978-88-544-1032-9

1 2 3 4 5 6   20 19 18 17 16

Printed in Croatia